Poems
of a
Spectrum-Autist

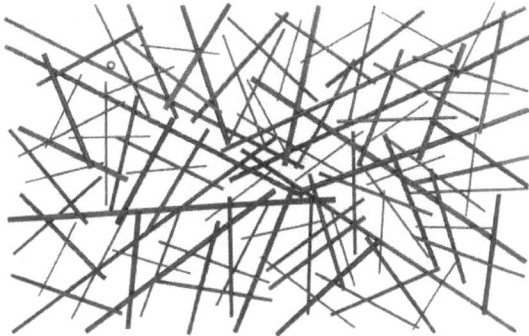

Marcus Holmes

$\mathcal{C}^2$

Parson's Porch Books

Poems of a Spectrum-Artist
ISBN 978-1-951472-10-8
© 2019 Marcus Holmes

Library of Congress Control Number:2019951158

Dedication

This monograph is dedicated to the memory of Doctor James Pallas and to my fellow autists who share this alternate way of being, wherever they are on the Spectrum.

I also dedicate it to all of those befuddled people who have put up with me over the years and endured the oddities of my otherness. You know who you are.

Table of Contents

7

PROLOGUE

The term Spectrum-Autist is how I describe one who is diagnosed with Autism-Spectrum Disorder. Since I do not think of Autism as a "disorder, I prefer "Spectrum-Autist." Being a Spectrum-Autist is to live in the in-between. In-between a typical person and a profound Autist. The in-between is a difficult place to be. People can see me both as normal and as strange. At first meeting me, there are not obvious signs and people often assume that I am like conventional humans. The more time they spend in conversation with me, however, that view can rapidly deteriorates, but they do not quite know why. They often recognize introversion, though I have been told by other introverts that I am "off the chart" introverted. For a while, "painfully introverted" suited me for a label. It is quite literally painful, to be among a group of people, expected to interact, and also to be alone, unable to be the person that I want to be. At times I thought that I would slip into deep autism, never to emerge. Meanwhile, I somehow got through school, college, graduate school, and a doctorate. I learned other languages as part of my educational requirements. Autistic people are not supposed to be good at language, right? It was only later that I discovered, with the help of a brilliant and compassionate psychologist, Doctor James Pallas, that I have (what was then called) Asperger's Syndrome. "What is that?", I asked. He first put it in simple terms. "You are a verbal-autistic." A verbal autist. Who knew? He took me through the diagnostic criteria, and it explained so much of my life, my behavior, and the way that I express myself.

Recently I reviewed poetry and prose that I had labored over across decades. The Autism Spectrum Disorder glared back at me and I saw my work in a new light. I offer the following collection all readers of poetry, but particularly those who seek to further understanding of the spectrum-autist mind and inner life. My autism has been a gift. While I often fail to recognize what typical humans recognize without effort, I have also found the transverse to be true. I have the ability to peer deeply and interpret uniquely. Because it can be a gift (to the point that some of us are called "savants"), I think of ourselves as being of an "alternative order" rather than as having a "dis-order." Though it is a mistake to assume we are all savants, which tends to be the image most portrayed on television.

People often mistake our stiffness or social awkwardness as being cold or uncaring. The opposite is true. Many of us are so intensely sensitive, so profoundly loving, that it must be contained. Something like anxiety resides in us and like a reflex, controls and limits our outward expressions. At the risk of sounding nerdy, the fictional character Spock is a classic example. His species is so emotional that they have had to develop techniques to suppress it just in order to function. I loved Spock as a child and related to him. I also cringed when other fully human people would encourage Spock to be "more human." They lacked a fundamental understanding of his species, of his order of life. In the words of Spock from Star Trek Into Darkness, "... you mistake my choice not to feel as a reflection of my not caring. Well, I assure you, the truth is precisely the opposite." For autists, the choice is imposed upon them.

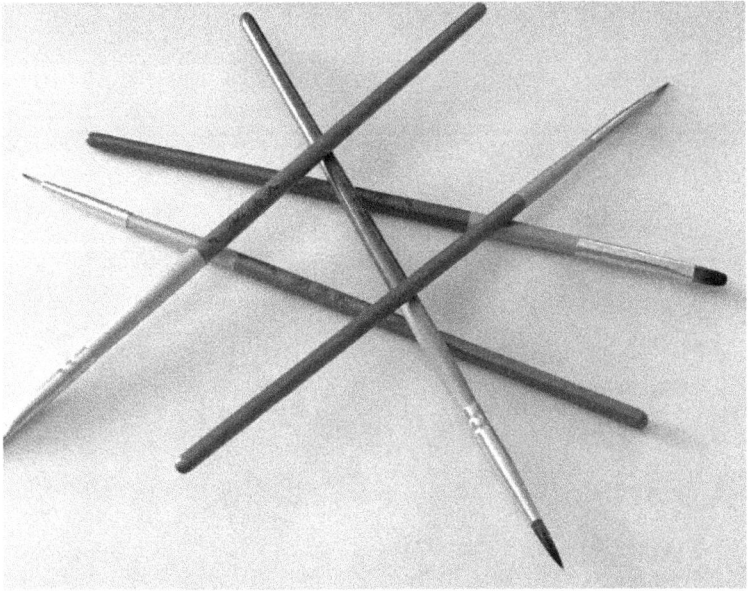

PAINTER

MY OWN SONG

I've got to have my own song
What on earth is life all about?
I think, but nobody listens
They just cry, they scream, and they shout
"Oh lord, help me. I'm in pain."

Dying. I'm dying to know.
Why are your feelings in despair?
Let me help you to ease your pain.
Let me show you that I care.
I just want to lessen your ache.

Dying to hear what's on your mind.
What's bothering you on this day?
I could help, if you'd let me try,
But you just sit there, and you say,
"Oh, lord, help me. I'm in pain."

Dying to hear the sweet music.
Where are we going today?
I've got some time on my hands,
So, talk all of your fears away.
I just want to ease your pain.

Dying to hear your own song.
What on earth is causing your fear?
I think I know, and I do care.
You just sit and sing through your tears,
"Oh, lord, help me. I'm in pain."

II. SIR, YOU ARE

Sir, You are the poet, not I!
I who paint my penciled lines, cry -
Grieve because my pictures lack the
Insight of... of your poignant scribbles.

III. A GREAT NATION

A nation is greatest when it is one with a world of nations.
One is greatest when he or she is one those of any stations
A nation is great when it welcomes those who are in danger
When one welcomes a stranger in need of a manger
A nation is great when it enacts God's will.
When one holds the ancient values, upheld by founders,
still.
A nation is great when it tears down walls.
When anyone can grace its streets and hallowed halls.

AUTUMN LAKE

You must understand something

> leaf to autumn lake

I see good in all individuals
Whether I like that human or not.

> lake current to falls

I tend to see the good in that human.
sometimes, however, one tries to show me
only the good, hiding the bad.

One might do this to protect me,
not wanting to hurt me,

> smile at the sun

Or one might simply be afraid to expose oneself,
afraid of rejection
Perhaps hide for fear that a friendship would be threatened,
or even come to an end

> falls to rapids

Portraying a perfect, nice human
Ironically, this is when the bad

> leaf decaying on the underside

is most often revealed to me.
a human like this must learn to trust me.

> rapids to cove

Such a human should try being totally and openly
honest with me.
> leaf to open sea

21

V. OF MUTES

We who are born as mutes
Hear. We cling to word-sounds
Find storms in our minds,
Quakes in our bodies,
But do not speak.
Dare not speak.

RIBBONS STRETCH

The ribbons stretch, the scotch-tape snaps,
And birthday-candled paper rips.
All while the heart, the lungs, and nerves
(And perhaps a trembling lip)
Asks "What's inside? I Wonder if…"
Then smiles and thank-yous and a quick
"What's next?" brings one more mystery.

VII. NEVER RULE

Rag-doll. Charmer.
Play that sun-cloud full.
Jesters in striped armor.
There's never been a rule.

CAUGHT

Caught on the number-line, counting...
days one, tow, six. Weeks two, three.
Months one, two, three, four, five, seven,
  nine   ten   el-   even
One year
always attempting to keep track.
for what? Why?
"Tender-loving care."
everything with a beginning
        must   have. an.   ending
enough of the number-line
one must find free-dom and fair-dom
or run a sinless race
to find false joy
within the limits of the number-line

UPON THE COLORS

Purpled orange.

        Black. Rainbowed. Oranged Purple.

Thus is the story   thus it is   the story

Where next will the brush touch

Upon the   colors?

How next   will the painter

land his   brush

Upon the   canvass.

Alive?   Sure.

Colors   fade, renew,

mix,   separate.

Dealing   them out like

marked   playing cards.

Painting an   indefinite - an

                                                                            ABSTRACT.

Center column inset:

Unseen   unseen
only motion only
motion sense direction.
color sensation deception
prevails
look-stimulus response
the wrong response! He's
blind. you
are blind too, looking back,
into the blurred colors of
him, the painter.

He who is not understood,

Only classified. different to every viewer.

Hiding in a darken, blurred sights

SUN SATURDAY

Awaking. warm blue nylon
Pulled over head to shield against cold night.
Pushed. Bright sunlight forces
Eye-lids shut, arms stretch.

Muscles and tendons and toes
Stretch legs across dusty roads.
Lake in sight, lake in sight.
Knees up, foot-bounce, gasp.

Sun glare white paper... eyes.
Meticulous note drawing, knees
Up, supporting wooden writing-board.
Paper flap in breeze ... mmm.

Breathe natural energy,
Trees resting, swaying, laughing,
Yawning, leaning over
Tissued bones of absorbing-me.

XI. CONVERSATIONS

"Yes, uh huh,"
Once upon a daylight merry
While I laundered wool and terry
"Right, I see."
Over many a loud-but-languid rotate
      Of an ageless dryer,
"Mm-hm, ya"
While I softened silken satin
Suddenly I saw a cat in
"wow, gosh"
Clover, grass and nip it sat in,
Sat in cat nip getting higher.
"Well sure, mm-hm."
"'Tis some feline there", I hollered,
Sat in cat nip getting higher,
"Listening? Sure, really. Go ahead",
Waiting for the stuff to fry her.

HE CALLS OUT TO HIMSELF

He calls out to himself but receives no answer.
Sitting on the tree stump he screams.
He searches with his eyes.
Beyond the hills, between, up, and around the trees,
Under, through and above the ponds,
And the door of the house never opens, or swings shut.

He searches with his tough
But only finds a worm, dark void...
An indirection to hurdle himself into...
If he could find himself.

XIII. EXTERIORLY

Stand exteriorly motionless.
Don't let anyone with crayons inside.
Did you talk to anyone today?
Smite desert. Hot, dry, grit.
Desert smite. Warm, moist, smooth.
Stand exteriorly motionless.

OPTICAL ILLUSION

Though it has a definite conclusion
This is an optical illusion.
It works to confuse the brain,
This zany, insane terrain.

You may pine, you may whine,
But don't decline, just define
This word of arbitrary vocabulary.

LEAVES

Sharp against blue, shade.
Crackle. dry-grass brushes,
Thumb-swept. sun flower
Seeds d
      r
      o
      p
  e   d on hot pavement.

MY JOB

My job is to be complete as I can be.
But I am nothing, but *this* cellophane.
All light passes through me.
Assaulting me is wind, sharp.
Assaulting me are sounds, many.

XVII. MOST DIFFICULT

Most Difficult
To find   those   few   words
Like choosing favorite stars
Out of a bright night sky
That would best fill
The blank white space
Of a photo's under

ECHO STRING

I left the blue upon a door.
You move string per my instructions.
How much are these colors worth
you   then   me
And when I'm seventy
Will the colors still live
Fade blend bright-a-fy
Well they remember, rejoice?
Muted are my words: share the silence.
Pronounced the temporary existence
Of humor shared.
Echo against the walls.
Echo to the walls.

XIX. BINDING THREADS

Pull hard
      binding threads
But please do not bleed today
      or in the future of yourself
Fall firm
      scraping skin
But please do not scream today
      cry here, quietly
With me.

SHADOWS OF NOON

The layers of the window at night
Fall lame to the shadows of noon
Then trumpets do sound in the light
And sailboats do dance to the tune

IN SCHOOL

In school every boy is told of the Siren Song,
And every one of them thinks it is about
Greek women, boats, rocks, and mysterious singing.

In life many men experience the Siren Song.
And every one of them learns that
All desire is a Siren. And we are our own undoing.

STONE

Three, in their wisdoms un-ease the stone.
In its peace it sits sturdy
wedged tightly comfortably high
upon boulders that seem to glide fast
As clouds race across a busy sky.
In its peace, the stone dreams beautiful
Dreams of colors, movements, sweet sounds.

There is the wind, who has her way to un-ease
The stone, blowing original winds,
Filling its cavities with her thoughts,
She stirs the dust that bury homes,
Sprats fine waters aboard sailing vessels,
Snaps tall, ageless tress from their roots,
Erodes the fiber of the stone.

Sun beams upon patina
Few direct beams stride. Most filter
Through autumn leaves, distorting light
Illuminating sight. She lights full a path
She travels brightening oceans
Tanning flesh, fading dark
Only a timid un-noticing light beams to the stone.

And here are the songs, gracing the stone.
These are songs of admiration, love, needs
For others. She never watches the stone.
The sons used to cling to wind for travel
And warm in the rays of the sun.
Now songs find their own paths, spreading
Young and awkward past tree, building and stone.

30

XXIII. DRAWING IN

Drawing in on myself
The world is tightening
water puddles shrink to drops
drawing in on themselves
falling, sinking into carpet
deep red, dark ocean big blue
the vacuum is tensing
collapsing in on itself
the air is too hard
I'm sinking too fast for the bends
crushing, falling in,
drawing in on myself.

ACROSS

Echo my breath across lake
Bring ears atoned to my ring
Dance along the water's edge
Gaze about the fire sky
Close warm hands around warm hands
And listen to the hilly walls
Echo my breath across lake.

SOME HUMANS ARE

Some humans are the Peace of night
some are the Peace of day.

Day Peace will
      tickle you
           pick you up and
                throw you about
      make you laugh and scream wildly with joy.

Peace of night will
      soothe you
           gently sway you sided to side
                hold you tight calm bliss
      to make you feel warm and secure

PINE AND PALM

Pine and palm
Reaching
Romance with stars

Cat in shadow
Hisses
At quiet emptiness

EYEBROWS

Crisp lettuce eyebrows
Rain upon my tears, red.
Running toward the finish-line.
One and two, flow-dancing
Through acid-rain clouds.
Purples and bow bring mountain peaks:
Rolling hills of purple felt
Lead high and long.

CLEAN YOURSELF UP

Clean yourself up,
You've got politics and peanut butter on your shirt.
This   day.
We'll be marching underneath,
Looking to the blue,
Watching for the rainbows in our hair.

A man in a white house
Loves the light
That cuts though the trees
And into our   e y   e s

It's just politics and sunshine,
Flowers in your hair,
Poly ticks and sunshine
Bombs bursting in air,
Po pop po litics tics ticks
and
SUN   SUn   Sun   sun shine.

33

XXIX. ENDLESS

Oh, hey! Do you see
The early morning sun?

Coordinate with accuracy
Your profoundidity light.
Express the endlessissity reach.
Let the seed groW.
Help seeds.

TOMORROW

Here tomorrow, standing in flower field,
Smelling scents in breeze carrying
Sounds of over-leaf-running rabbit.
Here tomorrow
Tomorrow
Do not make me leave you behind.
Do not send away my cotton shirts,
Blue unicycle shoes,
Smiles, stretched, with hard swept back,
Some tangled in forehead,
Eyebrows, by breeze brushing
Face, cheeks.
Here tomorrow
Tomorrow.

XXXI. EARS OF CORN AND EARL GREY TEA

Ears of corn and earl grey tea,
Elk Meat and English Toffee,
Eccles cakes and etouffee,
Egg-foo young and Blintz souffle,
Leafy salad, entrecôte,
Eastern oyster, escargot,
Blueberry waffles, empanadas,
Edamame, Enchiladas,
Eel and chocolate eclairs,
Edam cheese and elephant ears,
PBJ and C, Eggie bread,
Eau de vie and spinach omelette
Raisin muffins and eggrolls,
Empire apples, escarole.
Glass of eggnog, cup of joe,
Eucalyptus, espresso.

REDUPLICATIONS

Points of interest upon plane.
Accomplishing reduplications by ear and hand.
Child stood in contemplation,
Leapt, landed carefully.
Accuracy counts. Miss and loose.

UNDER

Under a blanket of passing clouds,
All he could think to say
When he saw the hunter
With rifle and cigar
Was
"You're noisy and disgusting."
In a not-S0-wild-life clearing
And fell asleep
Under a blanket of passing clouds.

MUFFLED VOICES

Dark mystery. Their muffled voices press
Against my ears. There's too much subtle stress.

ALL

Rules, guidelines, mutual understandings
Do not yell in libraries
Personal needs, wants and infatuations
Tea with lemon, please
Invade upon and are products of
All our lives

UNDER THE INFLUENCE OF B-SHARP

David is under the influence of B-sharp,
An alternate spelling of C.
He thinks this way when playing the harp,
And now the F-flat is an E.
Double A-sharp is a B, and double F-sharp is a G,
Now that he's begun, he cannot stop.
C-flat is a B, and double C-sharp is a D.
His mind is a music workshop.

XXXVII. ART

Cat, wide-eyed on a purple carpet,
Lying by a two-plated table.
Double-wedge bench, wooden, beneath.
He and She, smiling red lips, dark hair,
Making house complete, like Mom and Dad:
Animal, food for together-meals,
Sitting on same side, close.
Sharing a home, this gift,
Art, drawings, self-expression, exception,
Affirmation of Us, ignites Home.

THROUGH RAIN

The numbers are unreadable through the rain
Pounding on the roof and hood.
Seeking   and yet motionless.
Excuse-bound. Now is an undetermined entity.
Sailboats in the sky swirl about themselves,
Meandering, catching the drifts of the wind
Of the disturbance   they never collide.
How many will become imbibe-mes tonight?
          have no more resolutions.
          must resolve themselves.
Do not hit your head on the bells. Do not
His your head on the bells.
You, up on the rock... do not confuse
Me.   Do not understand the customs of your minds
Sit upon the stone close and yet detached.
Warm-wind blowing, staring at all one can see
Playing a nocturn in the trees and across the electrical
wires.
The used-to-be stars glow.
Blackness of the iris, eternal,
Sparkling reflections of the night-lit-sky
In the eyes of those who are close.
Warmth pacifies emotions
intertwine   combine   do not
confuse me anymore, you on the rock,
don't fall me by your name. That is not
Mine.
They strive to find oneness, though
There is no such existence. Schools
Flocks   families   One is an
undetermined   One minus point five
You do not know   cannot know
Yet you are not clouded

You are not crowded
        reach
But you cannot catch
        clasp   for
     fractionizers are not whole.
                  yet
Disturbed   perturbed.
You do not know
     cannot feel the unpleasantries
        extreme pleasantries
        delights
Of reaching, teaching, knowing
You've caught the string in your hand.
Orange dots   absence of communication,
Doors closing to the stars
            interaction of ourselves.
Orange dots: interval of time, traverse
To the peace   purposes of escape.
Frog swimming deeper, away from the threat of the deadly
bat...
     achieving temporary inner-peace
     developing growth
Slice of time, known as absence
          others may know as
A temporary journey... not vacation.
Yellow turns to wood in the black-light.
As not all days are bright.
Shadows on the wall appear, all five,
And all my eyes will follow their indirections.
They will sail around mind and beyond
The   feeble limitations.
Stand separatingly tall and relaxed,
Listening to the pounding on the roof, for
Even the numbers are unreadable through the rain.

INK-SHOT EYES

Give him fire
And he'll burn the world

Hear the voices yelling   screaming
        Filling up he precious head

Blood is dripping
Out his ball-point pen

Taste the sugar
On his grape-fruited lips

Watch the fire burn
Watch the growing glowing glare
        In his ink-shot eyes.

SITTING IN THE CLASSROOM

There are twenty-three desks
Ninety-two desk legs
Twelve panels of fluorescent lights
In three rows of four
The area of a triangle with a height of three
        and a bass of four is six,
Because half of twelve is six, and because
One half the base times the height of such a triangle is six.
Three squared times four squared is one hundred forty-four
        and the square root of one hundred forty-four is
twelve,
        and that is the hypotenuse.
Hypotenuse sounds like a cousin of Hippopotamus.
Hippopotamus literally means River Horse.
Why don't we call horses hippos?

I'm so hungry that I could eat a hippo.
There are two visible door-nobs in this room.
One on door to the hallway, and one on the bathroom door.
I hear the clock ticking, even though the other kids are
      loud screechy aliens who do things that
      I don't understand, and they speak phrases
        that adults don't, and I don't.
I prefer being with adults.
      They're calmer and they speak normal language
        most of the time.
The clock is round, like a pie pan.
      And it measures, like pi can.
I hate school.
      I want to go home and get back to my projects.
      It's eight steps from my desk to the door,
        except when we line up single file.
        That's so inefficient!
The teacher says that after recess
      we're going to do finger-painting.
Why would I want to paint my fingers?
I don't like to have stuff on my hands,
      not even gloves or mittens.
      Stuff on my hands is too loud for my skin.
The ceiling fan with six blades is too loud too.
      Not too loud for my ears.
        Too loud for my eyes.
The fan measures like the pie fan.
      One blade goes all the way around for each clock
click.

XLI. THE STRANGER VISION HERE

The stranger vision here
breathes golden light
listing waves crawl from dreams
Five voyages don't reach the bridge
Lure, struggle, clang space
glory glints glory, sleep tight

TAKEN BACK

Staring
At the quiet lake
Listening to the distant sounds
In the trees
Bats overhead
Reflect the glowing moonlight
Like falling stars, they fly

I'm taken back
In memory,
To times of long ago
Amazed by the summer night
It never changes
No

Lonely summer nights
Sitting at the water's edge
Alone
Warm slow breeze

I'm taken back
In memory
To times of many friends

Thinking of what times we've had
And why they had to end

Singed
As a moth is
By a flame
Crushed
As a soul is
When dreams die
A passive scene
To sit within
This mountain lake
In the sky
So still it sits
Without a sound
Sleeping
Through the night

So silent
This sleeping giant
And so loud are my thoughts
Rolling
To the water's edge
Then taken
By the warm winds
To diminish
Dispersing above and across
His yawning watery mouth

Trapped
In a world I cannot leave
Alive
In a world of memories

Every year
A lake to gaze at
Every year
This world to see
Every year
A summer night
Opens up these eyes
Opens up my cluttered mind

I'm taken back in memory
To places that I've been
Dreaming
Of those humaned places
I want to see again.

But now I sit
In company
Of past and present
Combined
Dreaming of a future day
When I'll be thinking of this time

Pain
Is caused by pressure
Yet I'm
Quite empty quiet inside
What is it, then,
That hurts me so?

Pressure
Is the stem
From a root
Of a warped perspective
Extending out
From the stem
Are branches
Of pain

One shouldn't hurt
From remembering times gone
One should rejoice
For the times
That have created
Those memories we blamed

So, I look upon
This water scene
With stars above small
Scanning
For those details
That touch me most of all

XLIII. ALL HALLOWS EVE

In the deepest dark extremes
Of my dim deranged mind
Lurk the shadows and the dreams
Of a very eerie kind.
I hear the hostile screams
And the painful, baleful whines
As they carry out their schemes
While far tolling bells do chime.

Wicked ones will roam untamed,
Getting gruesome as they go.
They won't even feel ashamed
When they burn they're favorite foe.
What a horrid little game!
Such an awful way to go,
Burning in the raging flame,
Blazing in the hot red glow.

In the chambers of my brain
Live the echoes of the dead,
They who haunt me but in vain,
And to kill the ones they dread.
'Tis a ghost with heavy chains,
Floating 'round without his head,
Leaving cold and crimson stains,
Bleeding, dripping blood of red.

"Let me be, you lifeless fiend!
Dwell about another site.
Could it be you intervened
Looking for a deadly fight?"
Demons, spirits, ghosts unseen,
Apparitions in the night,
Come to taunt me in routine,
Out to elevate my fright.

Waiting by the glowing blaze,
They must gaze there all-consumed
As they sit in morbid praise
Of eternal death and gloom.
Cursed are my few last days.
All my dreadful life is doomed.
They won't cease to haunt and haze
Until I lie within my tomb.

MUSICIAN

There was a man with an ear for vibrations,
He adlibbed, sung and composed incantations.
The man had a beard, red and long.
He had that kind of face that is bold and strong.
His legs were long like that of a stork
Yet he was chunky, somewhat like a pork.
Give him some time, a paper and pen,
He'll give you the world through his musical Zen.
He cooked his black notes in a caldron like stew
And threw them together, his musical brew.
With wand in his hand, and a pulse in his heart
He dreamed up the music he wished to impart.
A hat on his head, retrieved from in the gutter,
His trousers and shirt handed down from his brother.
This was creator of organized sound,
Though he was as well dressed as the neighborhood clown.

AWARENESS

Awareness is the key for you.
Don't shy away from all that's new.
Go show the world you have a care
And live your life, each day aware.

NATURE'S COLLAGE

When I was born into this world
I just had no idea.
The splendid mirth that fills the Earth
From Richmond to Korea

Life around this concrete4 ground
Is really quite a dream.
The birds, the rain, and everything
Make quite a wonderous scene

Well life's just great, accommodate
This positive entity.
Just envisage nature's collage
From Europe to Tahiti.

XLVII. I DID: I

Dear, dear Dad, I did: I
Pushed the lawn-mower
Hither and thither and even beyond

I sit within the sounds and sensations,
Past city and forest and day and night.
My presence in essence of life.

Fine cut grass, so proud, I see,
While laying out on beach-towel, under
Sunlight on green, in euphoric harmony.

DEEP, COOL

Canoe's   glide-brush

             .   .

     .

       deep, cool   w   e
                     a   t   r   ,
like   dUCks   I
                     O.

    .   .

     .

                  up.
           es
A branch reach

PUDDLES

Puddles in back with a wave goodbye.
Miss view ... miss view.
Ear voice again
Strong, mature, soul and body.

Mists condense to glass of water.
Miss view ... miss view.
Spin worlds together
Dance and I, words, flesh, color.

OF PINE

Days continue to pass us by.
Goodbye yesterday.
Wood and grass blades.
Steel blades in wood.
Rust   pulp   smell
Of rotting pine, oak, redwood.
Maggots   Suppertime!

ÉMINENCE GRISE

There have been in my life those who filled the role
Of éminence grise, angle on the shelf, advocate.
What value can one claim until one makes the goal
Not as a star, not even seen, a simple presence moderate.

THATAMAZING?!

Isn't thatamazing?!
Nearly seven billion individuals, and
No   where   to go.
Now here a friend sits away
        Yet in sight
As if to say, "Look!
"You sent me away. Look!
"Feel good now? Huh?
"You   hurt   me."
But this beauty will take care
        Of all your problems.
It mends! It blends!
It'll even tell the time!
Call now at 555.NOW.HERE
        And get a second one FREE.

LIII. I LET MY ROBIN FLY

I let my robin fly
I let my robin fly away from me.
We didn't even wave goodbye.

I let my robin fly
I guess that means my robin's free.
Fly high, my robin, bravely fly.

π

: Pi

A SHIP FLOATING

I see a ship floating away
Making its way across the bay
The humans on board are cheering
Some of the humans are tearing
They're leafing to go on a trip
On out of this world they will slip

I see a woman who's crying
I know what this is implying
The wind is gusting harder there
Brushing her wind-blown hair

There's a shallow voice in the wind
Calling. Crying. Then the exscind.
It was the girl's name that I heard
It was a most beautiful word
That singing ringing through my mind
That name that the girl was assigned
I'll not tell her name, though so true
There's not a reason to tell you

Beside her and holding her hand
Is a man in total command
Of himself and the way he acts
'he knows how to deal with the fats
He's a man of faith and passion
With dreams or new and old fashion.

Together they stand heart to heart
For these two do not want to part
Pouring her tears on his shoulder
"it's only healthy" he's told her.
They're beginning to osculate
Believing their love is their fate.

On a journey that will not cease
They go to an island of peace
They hope to find utopia
Or a at least a similar idea

The clouds are growing dark and strong
About to sing their mighty song
Soon we'll see a heavenly show
Lightening that will make the sky glow
It's a power like no other
An energy rush to smother
All concepts of doubts so intense
About life and death's prevalence

Under the immense rayless sky
This couple in love seems not shy
Standing on the deck all alone
Daring to confront the unknown
That lies in their long lives to come
Open to all of life's spectrum.

A seagull's flying aimlessly
Across the open tameless sea
Wandering lost yet shamelessly
Because it is a game to be
Free of a name and free of fame
Free to claim, the world's it's domain
The ship is a spec in a pool

Like a link in the chain of a fool
A white dot amongst many seen
Like a star in tits speckled scene

Though so small as this ship may seem
Out on the boundless ocean dream
The regal seagull found its way
To that great ship where it will stay.
It is circling now high above
Gliding downward with the ease of
A single feather in the air
The gull has perched to guide a prayer.

Four eyes once glowing, gleaming strong
Once almost chanting, singing song,
They now are settled questioning
One pair of seagull eyes peering
At their youthful human figures
There's much to learn from harbingers.

The angry waters toss and spit
Like a crying child in a fit
Storms and roars, yet it's just a skit
This day it will display its wit
But later it will rest a bit
And peacefully it will just sit.

A risen wave descends upon
The deck, then spreads, and soon is gone
The crescent wave has carried much
There in its large and mighty clutch

There's a product of the crashed wave
Sitting soaked from its wet grace
It is a white rose sweet as milk

As strong yet smooth and soft as silk
The curious couple still stare
At the gull witty the glowing glare
Not noticing the lustrous rose
That lies there as the ocean chose

As yet the showers have not poured
And the black-cloud sky has not roared
No lightening streaked or flashed abroad
Upon these lives no storm has trod
Only signs of the storm-to-be
Haunt all life with its energy.

Now the dreamers, young eyes follow
While through the breeze the gull does flow
Like a magician's gliding hand
The gull flew with a grand command
Soon it's landed with great skill
The couple watching, standing still.

Finally, the tension ceases
Though the nerves were torn to pieces
One streak of lightening bolted bright
Across the sky with voltage might

Then suddenly the gull was seen
To snatch the rose up by the green
And sturdy stem. It then took it
To the girl whose face was still lit
By love's sweet glow that never quits
Upon her arm the gull now sits
To present the lustrous flower
With a most alluring power
The gull has disappeared. It's fled.
The rose is limp and brown. It's dead.

Only the beloved couple
Still stay secure yet supple.
Into their cabin they must go,
Just prior to the flitting show.

LAKE

Drilling tip into a swirl of marble:
Orange-flowered ice-cream clouds re-twisted.
Center-punctured, they bleed their white bubble-
Forming hard-wind catching said (now wind caught)
For the cloud has let its bleeding, as rainbow,
Down the loose-cork sky-erected timber.
It sails into its dream-wished ocean

Toward the over-sized and loud reflections:
Bobbing of the sunlight grouped spackles,
Disappearing re-appearing   hungry
Magic tricks abound about the surface.
Water swallowing   replenishing   and
Then regurgitating for the happy

Smile-stretched curiosity between the
Waxy ears of one whose red-hair
Brightly shines as of the burning embers.
Bread is flung into the water ripples:
Some will sink, but most will float to hungry
Beaks not far away   and gamey fish.
Wave hello to passers-by. Aloha.

ISLAND OF THIRTY-SIX

Island of thirty-six like-minders
Dwelling on each other   feedingon
Their situation is unique (?),
For they dwell in the after-spelling
Spilling   drillingtwisting   distorting.
          now   now   now   now
Eat, love, sing, and manufacture delight.
Fourteen every-do-appearance of the sun -
And such an occasion with the moon.

COCOON

Public leg-twisting lessons.
Disguising to fill gaps from absent one.
Fill in as let (drive) out.
Plague of an incomplete sound sharing experience.
Welcome, friend. Don't leave here.
If the two are one, then two minus one equals zero.
Cocoon warmth *my* with *your*.

WHERE AM I TO LAND?

Where am I to land?
мне суждено замерзнуть?
A dust-filled polluted
Transparent carcass,
Attached, mixed and undefined
Somewhere in the frozen lake
Cold eternal death
Cold eternal body
Forever forgotten

One of wide white-rapid rivers
Many miles long, meandering,
Flowing toward unseen falls
Or an unseen ocean.
Caught in a whirlpool.
Eternal life of sorts.
Eternal body or soul?
Forever forgotten?

Am I to find a sun?
Dispersing, reaching for sky
transparent others around me
ascending easily one path descended
the other side of the escalator.
Anti-gravity pulls.
Metamorphosis of soul.
Metamorphosis of body.
Forever forgotten

LIX. REACHING

Grabbing rainbow tails.
Golden sun-blond smiles
From behind soft vails,
Reaching through thick miles.

I'M THE MAN WITH THE REED IN HIS MOUTH

Show me some copper or silver or green.
Put a quarter in my case
I'll play a fast lick for you.
You can find me by the pier
From eight a.m. tell seven at night
Unless a badge tells me to
Find another spot.

I must be good enough for a coin
From a passing nod,
But not good enough to gather a crowd.
I'm the man with the reed in his mouth.
Put a nickel in my pocket and I'll play for you,
Watch the wrinkled old man turn blue for you

LXI. ALMOST ANYONE

Almost anyone who looks like almost anything
would look like he or she belongs here
one with his tight holes tank top t-shirt
muscles well-conditioned.
one well-dressed carrying several
nearly unmanageable books.
some clump together in groups
of two or more,

Some sit or stand alone   very
         alone
                they think
many form long noise-filled confusing lines
leading to unseen fortunes.
many scatter among the bricks
und finden sich ein Teil der Menge,
adding to the confusion, the noise,
and lack of   space

RESTING ON

Resting on a white-bordered slab
Of old Kodak paper.
Smiling into worlds
Beyond my mind.
Caught in the gentle cautious grasp
Of my lonely hand.

I WENT TO PHYSICAL EDUCATION CLASS

I went to Physical Education class today
And learned that my contemporaries are aliens.
Coach said we were going to play football.
I became a little excited to learn about this sport,
My anticipation grew until it suddenly vanished,
Just as it had with baseball and Soccer and Track and
Field...
When he said that we were to choose teams and
Have a go at it. ???

What happened to the Education part?
How does one hold a football?
What are the rules of the game?
Where do I stand?
Where do I go from there?
Is there special language I must learn, special skills?
How can we just have a go at it if you don't tell us anything?
But the other boys had a go at it, as though by magic.
But I was lost.   Had I missed a day? The day when the coach
Taught them all?

STILL I AM A CHILD

Still I am a child,
But growing, changing
With each day, each hour.
Every aspect of my soul
(mind, power, heart)
Stimulated be the life
And the death
That surround me.
Still I fall
Like a drop of rain.
I'm not an individual,
Not lonely.
I journey among others.
I am free
To live, share, love.
I am uncomplicated,
Simple as life itself.

DROP OF RAIN

I am but a child,
Inferior, untamed.
Like a falling drop of rain,
I am an individual.
Lonely, free, simple.

NO LONGER ONE OUTSIDE MYSELF

I am no longer one outside myself.
I live, I breathe, but most of all I feel.
I used to lie outside a foreign world.
All day I'd peer in, through the glass between.
Observing every move that humans make,
I'd try to understand just why they do
The things they do, and why I'm not the same.
And through a medium – my body self,
I was among the others - I was not…
Of them. So, *They* and *I* was never *We*.
I worked to find a reason for all things,
Like love and life and time. I studied hard.
I'm old beyond my earth-lived age, I'm told.
But I am young, I've learned, like life itself.
I am no longer one outside myself.
I live, I breathe, but most of all I feel.

LXVII. THE BIRDS, THEY SING

The birds, they sing real loud
And when they do,
Prized thoughts of you
Appear in my mind, and cloud.

Mem'ries of past times ring.
Some recall fun
Occasions, some
Remember the birds. They sing.

I WALK IN NEVER-ENDING CIRCLES SEEKING TRUTH,

I walk in never-ending circles seeking Truth,
Accumulating facts and observations.
But I come to no conclusions as I sleuth.
The more that's clear, the more that's obfuscation.

SHOULD NEED TO BE COMPELLED TO BE OBLIGATED TO

Should need to be compelled to be obligated to
Or have got to, ought to, have a choice to do
What I think is best, what I think is correct,
What I think I knew to express respect.

Got to do not naught to do what wrought to do
What thought to do because I was taught to do
What I'm supposed to do, what I want to do.
Should I need to do what I need to be to be free?

GRASP, AND THEN LET GO OF EVERYTHING

Grasp, and then let go of everything.
Catch the fish, if you must, then release it into its home.
Find someone to love, and then let them go when it's time.
Eat the meal on the big round plate of existence
And then digest it and pass it.
Know everything and then let it pass to instinct.
Know nothing, for you are a humble student of life.
Unlearning is the essence of learning.

LXXI. OH, OLECRANON

Oh, Olecranon, you serve me well.
You bend my arm when e'er I must,
But how, Olecranon you hurt like hell.
It isn't funny when you get percussed!

STAYING ON THE BALL MEANS TRYING NOT TO FALL

Staying on the ball means trying not to fall,
As your feet flail and your legs kick
And your arms outstretch tilt like wings on a plane,
Hips and ribcage do a dance in the middle,
And all you want to do is pay this month's bills.

LXXIII. HILL-CLUNG

Hill-clung fog settled under sun
Anticipation   livestock changeover
                                        greet travelers of time
                                                              area
                        searchers of humankind
                                                         change
              similarity in individual uniqueness
Return from long journeys   new
Journeys begin   find   find

RUN DOWN STAIRS

Crisp and sharp is the early morning air
One finds a need to rush with utmost care
You can take a hot shower if you dare
But you'll freeze until you blow-dry your hair.

You run down stairs to eat your morning meal
Nothing much, just some juice and toasted heel
Then drive to work to get the feel
Of headaches that the doctor says aren't real

It is amazing all that you've acquired
Finally the working day has expired
You start the car up though you're very tired

Time for heavy traffic and noise so cruel
Day in, day out you've got to keep your cool
You come to think that you may be a fool
Living life like every day's your last dual

Finally, you pull into the driveway
Happy that you've lasted one more tough day
Your home is like a soft, single sunray
And sits still to hear what you have to say.

INSTEAD, SAINTED

Instead, sainted, defiant or fainted,
Trashed threads, or an allergy gallery,
Reacted or created, or players replays,
Stories of sorties, or an optical topical,
Be altered and related, praised and aspired,
Observe the obverse, wage a potter's protest.
Regally and largely belay hardest hatreds.

OF LOVELY MINDS*

Lofty walls are painted yellow.
Poor he does his tasks too mellow
And he hears her speaking, ringing
Gentle soft and subtle singing
Of her mellow tongue-told thinking.
And the paint then peals away.

Flowers stand upon the table
Still he finds himself unable
And he sees her shadow standing
Lucid, gleaming, reprimanding
In his teasing mind demanding
And the flowers wilt away

_____

* after reading Poe's Raven

Shining rainbows fall from heaven
And the clock tolls half-past seven
Reaching out across creation,
Reaching in anticipation
Of her ghostly adoration.
Rainbows plunge into the bay.

Cats are swiping at the shadows
So that everyone who's mad knows
No one stands before him, dreaming,
Warm hand reaching, white teeth gleaming,
And the cats engulf their prey.

BRIGHT ROUND LIGHT BEAMING FROM HIS "GOOD" SIDE

bright round light beaming from his "good" side
a spot-light
       flash-lightening caught and frozen
          in prime of life
only to die by a flip of one
      small   simple plastic black switch

cold conditioned air, blowing from behind
freeze shoulders   spine   neck
        while the sheeted feet sweat in response
     to humid   hot-tempered nights.

this and the propped pillow
fine feathers squished and reshaped
       suffocating between one heavy back
       and one oaken-beam bed head-board
now become an arm-rest and back-breaker bar.

these, and the "Wonderful Cities" anthology
sitting open, sunk into his lap
as he reads, "Cats and Dogs and Postmen Fly, They"

Cats and dogs and postmen fly, they
Flee, they float, and taste the air, but
Still they'll breathe their hazard breaths 'till
Rain and hail and fog and mountain
Air make clear their senses limits

Poisoned river campers' baths and
Napalm in the radar-clouds and
Winds sweep by "the company",
Chimneys, oh, great Jimminies! Oh,
Save the whales and chimpanzees and
Find a cure for broken hearts and
Minds and lungs and smiles and eardrums.
Flying, falling, feelings, fleeting,
Senses limited by clouds for
Cats, and dogs and postmen also

and the light shines its inverse-shadow
across and beyond his reading body
          his back-beat, head-tilted, eye-burning body
                    and onto the wall on his other side.
The blue spot-light-glowing wall radiates one
          large black image of a reader.

one easy turn of the page of the book
that bleed that so entrances his curious mind
          and the black image, tired eye.
he stops to observe this curious figure who
dares to stare back, watching, mimicking him.

the dark image slowly, clumsily falls
a crumbling tree
      a ship sinking into the forever distant horizon,
          glowing, fading,
only to appear again with yet one more such flash.
One small, simple, plastic black switch clicks.

FROM THE LORDLY HEAVEN

From the lordly heavens towering above my brain
He reached out his hand, strong, muscular, warm and
skillful.
His magical grasp clenched mine, firm yet gentle
As a father shaking the hand of a five-year-old child.
A god for so long, now reduced to a mere magnificent man.
Standing before me in bright human clothes, grey human
hair,
Fine, stately, respectful, well-contoured, strong and
distinguished
          Yet gently human face
Looked with friendship into my face and boyish content.
Later I was to receive with hoy a fulfillment, eagerness
finalized,
      His human long exercised hand, long
      Exercised   signature   that I
should
      Keep for my life with pleasure   in black ink
      With my pen!
Will be ever known (did, does he) the excitedness with
which I
      Now fulfilling life?! Because of him
      And our about – time acquaintance.

LXXIX. RADIANT

Radiant Rebecca took a swim in warm water.
A jelly-fish brushed up against her ankle.
The sting started getting hotter and hotter.
She stepped in some rocks and got her foot tangled.
When she freed herself, she climbed up on the shore.
Her foot was gushing red gooey gore.
She passed out there upon the sand.
This wasn't the vacation that she had planned.

I'M TRYING TO EXPRESS MY ME

I'm trying to express my me instantaneously,
But I'm often urged (against my will) toward the feelings
Others have when attempting rapid from-in-to-out
Expressions in sound
            facial contusions
            the bend of standing body   absorbing
All the shakings   giving shakings   so,
So busy out-putting   so much energy-making.
Rumbles   air (low) rushes   round reverberations
high
And tumbling low, warming ear-side of body,
E e e e e a. a a yoe op high-to-low then shakings cease.

HEAT'S DOWN

Heat's down. Gather wood.
Burn the newspapers!
Cats crawl over shoulders, pat face.
"Dump the trash" announces the third.
Welcome home, advisors.
Talk to me. Involve in me.
Rejoice in our us-ness.
Play for me. Be for me.
Express for the us in me-and-you.

ONE LOVING PUN-KITTEN, EYES LARGE

One loving pun-kitten, eyes large,
To follow me to undermined places
Wake me in the thunder night, with arms
Climb into the human of my gentle morning purge
Cling to eyes with big face, happy
Accompany me in my meals at the table.

LXXXIII. RAINBOW

Rainbow
Arching through stone.
Light-waves
Bombarding body.
Flesh eats steel.

THE SILENT SHALLOW BREATHS

The silent shallow breaths of those who rest
Attempt to recreate a gentle breeze
While 'neath the cool and quiet darkened sky
An ambulance sends whining warning sounds
to all who care to hear... or lie awake.
when twirling red lights light the window panes
and in a ghostly glare speed down the street,
illusioning a sharp bright bow of red,
the humming engine's heard (the siren's off)
But still the sound of brushing air is there
against the wheels, white body, and the lights.

THE GOODBYE NIGHT

Giant mice, dogs, furred creatures,
Plastic mountains, men with no minds,
Translucent dancers scream from above,
And the lights growing into the night.

Diminished fifth symphony, chords dripping wet,
Algae and rowboats   no control.
Lunar trips and falls and spins and shouts
'Til everyone finds a favorite today.
Houses in trees and insects and homes
In the hearts, the castles, the heads –
All the heads three-feet tall (big eyes)
Two feet large   they talk on.

Blue skies, red, clouded, clear, bright,
But never polluted just haunting or happy
To every small child who cares to look
Past a monogrammed, feathered, illustrious,

One Day Only, bright and alluring hat.
"Mom!" crying, searching through tears
Eye-burning some young loud monotonous
Temperament child clutched in the arms
Of one furry, giant, five- and one-half foot
           MOUSE

Green, red, yellow, rainbow papers to lands
Far away, never nearby - always a walk toward
"I think it's in that direction. Where's the map?"
Lovely I the crowds – the loud, large,
(growing smaller toward night) crowds.
Submarines, bubbles, fish, plastic coral,
Exposed buried treasure of worth
To the wondering fantasy mind. Crowded.
"We're under water!" about six feet down.
Mechanical mermaids who don't short-circuit.
Divers for show in black and blue bruised suits
           No pirates here.

Music, sounds, colors, humans, animation,
This land, that land, and the one in between.
Illusions, confusions, thrills and chills.
Safaris, ghosts, pirates, and butterflies
Tired, aching feet, and one long, long,
Strenuous walk into the goodbye night.

I NEVER NOTICED

I never noticed them before.
The plaster creases overhead.
It fin'ly happened with me numb.
just hours before my brain awakes.

my funny head - no balance - fell
from high above the pillar neck
to swing, to rest, to look above.

to dizzy me. I too must sway.
My heavy hanging skull will fall
My body to the soft shag rug -
The room is lovely, bright and round
but I must fall and spin to ground,
And hope that I will wake profound
And hope that I will wake profound.

USING THE WRONG WORDS. THEY'RE RIGHT TO ME

I use the wrong words. They're right to me.
A kid and his friends at school are bullying.
I call them "hoods".
They laugh at me and mock me. "Hoods?"
I don't know why.
I ask them for a more appropriate word.
They shake their head, laughing, and walk away.
I am left not knowing what word to use.

ONE USUALLY FINDS

one usually finds difficulty breathing
when the heart is in one's throat
one of a few scratches on the barrel
yet one of many to come
the good doctor examined me
his conclusion is yet to come
the lawyer delved into my recollections
the verdict is you to come
the analyst delved into my past
where do I stand among the others?

LXXXIX. ECLIPSE

He will say, "It says here that
It   Was   Spectacular,
A once-in-our-lifetime experience.
And I missed it - wasn't even born yet."
Oh, it was. "Did you see it?"
I watched it, in peaceful calm,
Coolness of night, black velvet sky
Filled with clear star formations,
My brain filled with ideas and heroes:
Einstein, Descartes, Poe, Beethoven
Mother and Father, Newton, God.
I watched it as its white glow
Brightened into a fine spec
And then disappeared,
Leaving only the warm glow,
Like the embers of an almost burnt-out campfire,
That millions of viewers shared simultaneously.
"But light travels at a constant,
So, no two saw it at the same time, really",
He will say.

SHAPE HUMANS

Humans shape humans
Everyone from businesswoman to house-husband
To soon-to-be guilty of moral hypocrisy baby.
Vulnerable innocent ones-children.
Shape them, selfishly, into images of ourselves.
Grow up and carry on ancient traditions.

Be open and uninhibited. Kneel. Listen.
Footsteps, laughter, drinking-fountain, wind.
Potentials of learning and existing honestly.
Break them of fear-habits.
Alright to be "wrong". Be.

THE SILENCE IN THE SUN-STREAKED SHADE

The silence in the sun-streaked shade
The scattered prim rainbow lights
And limp at on the window-sill
Await the dimming dawn of dusk
And sleeping in the dark blue chair
Am I, beside my warming drink.

A silver clip shines brightly while
A two-foot creeping shadow, dark,
Is cast in deepest honor of
The fat-haired ball-point plastic pen
Straight-standing, vertical, tip-high,
Within its carpet-lodged black cap.

IN THE CROSSWORD PUZZLE (I DON'T FIT.) OF LIFE

In the crossword puzzle (I don't fit.) of life

SOLILOQUY FROM THE UNWRITTEN PLAY

Unsure, I live on in mighty god's hands
Her fingers stretching out, seemingly endless
As I sit mesmerized by her beauty, power, mystery.
I am a man-farmer who gazes at the splendor of his fields
Complexity of soft wheat stalks, shapes and shades puzzled
together.
Simplicity. To open one's eyes and stretch one's lips
In a grin, for the beauty of the power of gold
As I sit, unsure, I live on.

A tear formed beneath his eye. It fell from my eye,
But it landed lodged where it belonged.
The tear should be his too, shared by us both.
I sat next to his body as I sit now unsure. I live on.
He was fascinated by colors and all that reflected light,
Or seemed void of color and light.
He'd find shapes in refracted light,
colors in those shapes
A new presence to glorify
A new excuse to smile at what yet he would never
understand.

~~~~~~~~~~~~~~~~~~~~~~~~~

~~~~~~~~~~~~~~~~~~~~~~~~~~~

~~~~~~~~~WAVES ~~~~~~~~

STRANGER

Tongue-washing chicken-fingers after waving
stranger drives through our brains
one game is lost after
another is successfully executed

VISIONS

visions obscured by space enclosed upon
stars giggle, adorn worlds
bathe in heat of breathing suns
yearn for life (blow to) coals
catch ablaze, filling space
burning? Waring? Reviving? Live.

HERE

Laughing in the right key,
(Smile into brown eyes, dear)
Dark but shining brightly
Artemis has come here.

XCVII. THE FUTURE

The future
Drags far behind me now
I've nothing
Of sure significance
To look forward to
Dreams became rank nightmares

Views and vicious visions
Were like the worm
Now they are but bird feces
Lying, drying
On yesterday's comic section.

BREATHE

Breathe, clap, sing.
Be recognized, possessive, selfish,
Reach for the balloon
Hovering above your head
but don't be too conspicuous
as you plunge a reed through its skin

      Breathe, clap, sing.
      Fear the wilting of your flowers
      grin into the pond like narcissus
      to push the sailboat to the sand
      securing your sun-gazing feet.

GOLDEN

Golden contrast in warmth melting cold.
Image crosses from frame to frame
Absorb the moisture
Scene into scene, they absorb
walk with me through the land
making tracks and patterns with ourselves
creating by changing, by molding
by being ourselves   golden

LIGHT-WRITES

Reminded by rediscovered light-writes
the bitterness has evaporated
I'd forgotten I felt that way once
curl up onto my mind and purr
scattered pieces form the picture
ride on sweet dreams
into the land of our future domain
let me be the link
between your branch and theirs
let us all appear in the same light-write.

CI. EVOLUTION

Post-historic evolution foreseen.
That caterpillar has not died. It's
Metamorphs into butterfly.
Swing high toward trees
Feel the leaves fall crisp,
Mount to ground, squish.
White dwarfs. Waves. Matter.
Energy in Hydrostatic Equilibrium.

LISTING

Listing nerve-benders
      Darkened glass
Ghosts stare out, reaching
      Darkened glass
Sharpened knives glitter
      Sheeted ice melted
Darkened glass

CIII. TOMORROW'S

Grow young. Grow old.
Mingle my mind through daze.
Dizzy me and calm to my
Lap tomorrow's Valentine.
Jagged heart, a jagged heart
Map tomorrow's Valentine.

WAVES

Go celebrate the waves
Drifting through
Dreamy days
Telling you
Nothing's ever new
So, celebrate the waves

CRAWL

Baby cry
Learning new crawl skills
(as seemingly pointless they may be)
chance of prolonged breathing, heart beating
may be achieved with effort
stumble, rise, reach

FROM BLANKETS AND ROPES

Build a house from blankets and ropes.
Shade all the light that comes in.
Serve the wine. Don't speak.
Try not to make too much noise.
The praying-mantis stands in calm
moments before his kill.

CVII. HERO

Onemind,manythoughts.
Skippingstonesonaclear,
Sahllowlake.Smoothstones,
Softagainstfeet,dryinhands.
Searchforgold,pan,look,
Sift.Heroofapastnoon.
Swiminmountainwaters,
Sunwarming,beamingbright.
Smallpoolsaccomodatedfriends.
Skindarkensinlight,bodies
Still,relaxing,aching
Soon.Iamthetender,loving
Serpent,swimming,gliding,
Slippingthroughyourfingers.
Oh,formyspecialfriendsagain.

DREAMS

Plans formulate
minds involve
clouds dissipate
salts dissolve

The fountain flows for dear and fawn
warm drops will tell us of the dreams
from forest and the early dawn
to starry nights by mountain streams

CIX. FLOWING

dense blue-greyness wetting lair
to forehead, eyebrows
soaking warm moist socks in
nylon no-running-today shoes
a Monday recapitulation,
actual development of last week's
exposition flowing over stones
gentle sparkling image-
making over-things stare
awaiting the ruffling breeze

FIVE MILE

Five mile white cloud.
Needle in compass
Spins unpredictably
Sounds burst the distance barrier

VOYAGES

Planning voyages across land and time
seeking kind acceptance
in search for images to satisfy
images receptors seek

DON'T PLEAD

Don't plead pink blossoms with me
Come to my store, though
Make a fair exchange, But
Don't plead pink blossoms with me.

CXIII. HOURGLASS

Stretched fishers, coarse across taught wire threads.
Deep vibrations penetrate the room's ears.
A healthy yet emaciated figure wraps itself around.

The hourglass tremble maker.
Sweetness sounds from swift sways of the taught hair.
Tantalize.   Consume.   Involve.

Short sharp regular strikes destroy air.
Still whines, wheel-braking tone, lasering
Through me I grow holes Swiss-cheesing.
I crackle as floor vibrates beneath
Around feet.

Poems of a Spectrum-Autist

The little girl pushes her plastic-doll-filled songs.
It's time for your nap. Want warm milk?
I'll jog the mile even if it kills mew.
Can't come out now - gotta practice.
Hello. I'm very nervous. OK. here-goes.

REACH

Align the apples and pears, sorting
juggling round ones
discarding jagged fruit, sour fruit
hang ribbons from trees
reach far, but don't touch

BRIDGE

Anxiety-filled by your impending presence
I shovel an empty path
a bridge that doesn't reach the other side
Send an invitation of sweat and fire

LURE

Stand tall and sure
your body lines
lit by moonshine
and as we dine
drink low the wine
then feel the lure
and you'll be mine

STRUGGLE

Millions of worms
slither through earth
billions of germs
struggle for worth
please send away the formal dine
but let us drink the dark sweet wine

CLANG

Clang clang clang clang clang
and hot water soaks the bubbles
purging, healing, comforting.

clang
a tree is drying in wind
brown boxes hibernate in dark

SPACE

Red plus blue is a purple sky.
One plus less equals two and more
where sharing is the goal
smiles into my eyes
laughs into my ears
and sense the growing space around us.

GLORY

Thrust into a disguised glory
watching the sun move beyond the curtains
becoming a star beyond the planets.

GLINTS

soon backing hints
still mysterious
moon-cracking glints
thrill-harmonious

GLORY, LET IT SHINE

Bring forth the glory and let is shine
as a rainbow beaming colors to the eyes
but don't be too dazzled.
Don't look too long or too closely
or you may blind by its beauty
realize the reality of your mortality
feel the warmth of its glow
with that you may grow.

SLEEP

Kitten squirms for warmth and cuddling
purr-vibrations.
Stay warm, eat, scratch, play, sleep, eat,
attack a spot of sun light on the carpet
eat, sleep, grow
wake, hop in a cardboard box,
hop out again, chase after nothing

TIGHT ROUND MARBLES SPIN

Tight round marbles spin
gleaming red blue life-breathing
breeze and hot coals glow

俳句

HAIKU or Low New High Cue

unusual off-
beat scatological wit
now independent

haikai-no-renga
to hokku's nephew haiku
sing from the mountain

CXXVII. MÜSSEN SIE DANN VERBRENNUNGEN

It's here again to tease the human mind,
To make the little children play the game
To breathe a gentle breath upon the flame,
And warm the hearts of friends so very kind.
Some sit alone and watch the day pass by.
They think that through they're free they're quite confined,
That they may very well be left behind,
That they'll remain alone until they die.
One year from now will nothing be the same?
Or will they once again sit still and sigh?
A long enduring day has left them lame.
It seems life's coldest on a holiday
For those whose hearts pound lonesomely away.

イオタ

listen carefully
clever wake-up alarm
playing "let it be."

open window breeze
opening a rigid mind
buzzing bees in trees

when the climbing-trees
and long green-grass-blade-splittings
are gone.   we are gone.

CXXXI. AM I A DUCK?

Am I a duck?
I'm living in
A dream-land, held
Between the gifts
Of dull-day right
And bright day dream
But who's to say
What's right or dream?
What's dream or wrong?

イオタ

nictitating membrane
the third lid of a shark's eye
polar bears, aardvarks

95

Poems of a Spectrum-Autist

ebullient truth
eschew equivocation
seize encomium

who reads poetry?
is it one who seeks deep mind?
world soul? a mirror.

イオタ

homographs: bank; file;
mean; dove; murder; intimate;
carp; lighter; story

I stand in the shade
of the planet earth in awe
eyes reflecting light

CXXXVII. FRIDAY

It is Friday. (so?)
Without today we would not have
tomorrow or today.

then there would be no worms in the
tomorrow that would not exist,

but only within yesterday's wet ground.
If there were no today, then there would be

a never-ending yesterday.
Then everything would either live

Forever or they would die
Forever, stuck in time.

Or, possibly,

Our everything would live in yesterday
(of which would really be today
if Friday never did arrive.)

———

gas spread in dim night
flames filled a gray nothingness.
now all are burning.

CXXXIX. EVERYTHING WENT

You may propose "anything goes"
In this rowdy month of May.
I don't suppose you would oppose
Trying it again someday.

I must confess you did progress
When it came right down to it.
You great success, I'd like to stress
Was do to fear and spirit.

With that play you're finished, clearly,
But you'll always have your mem'ries.
Hence forth we'll get large crowds yearly,
'Cause they'll know we aim to please.

———

Hipponactean
iambic trimeter in
simple choriambus

イオタ

callipygian
stranger on a speeding train
cage and disengage

ululating wolf
under full resplendent moon
songs of wilderness

98

Poems of a Spectrum-Autist

ecce homo hangs
suffering, despair, guilt, shock
empty cross stirs hope

イオタ

the fire in full blaze
shudders fearful and anxious
glorifying life and death

relentless power
a presence construed as god
feelings we call love

yellow butterflies
eat the brown peanut butter
in dry-bird-bath park

イオタ

prancing pheasant trees
rising wavy heat impairs vision
steam split green lawn roots

always wise eyelids
gaze on vague horizon shines
from the dying dawn

CXLIX. THAT'S ALL RIGHT, REALLY

That's all right, really if
You *want* to believe
Skies are painted blue with sun,
Beam-bright strong at us.

(And) It doesn't matter, really if
You're out of *touch* with…
Arm(s mind f)olded into a
Brown paper bag every weekday

Round and round SHE goes Where
She lands… she doesn't even…
"No. Tell it to me straight."
Wait till you see the white of

Her teeth in that head-round,
With What Hair! Long, smooth,
Past (far) shoulders and skin-taught
Spiny back and sharp smooth blades

(Let) your mind to slumber cycle:
Skies are gone and spinning's fine,
Provided free ballet movement
Through the colors, sounds, finger tips.

———

sun-heat beat flat rock
arched branch let go as breeze blew.
swim low in the tears.

CLI. 1 5WEET 1

5weet 1, I am allowed mistakes, aren't I?
I'm sorry, truly, for these things I said.
I found myself embarrassed - thought I'd die.
I found a pair of shades upon my head.
Polaroid sunglasses.

What's worse than shadows that aren't really there?
What's worse than finding out your facts are fraud?
Not knowing if your friend's aware you care,
And knowing that said friend lives far abroad,
Loneliness - no time lapses.

> she smiled large and loud
> until the sight of no one
> filled her dreaming mind

I am not lost here
walking through the forest wind
free to dance with friends

> visions taking shape
> smooth. round. jagged.
> bird in flight

inexorable
hushed presence construed as god
passions we call love

> snow-crisp mountain breeze
> final effort to reach sun
> leave mountain-fog ghosts

CLVII. DOTS BLURRED

Yellow-orange dots upon the atmosphere blurred distinctly
air.
Red chutes of grass bamboo propel toward
Swing-sets and kiddy-knee dirt from
Brick walls grow it hard, course. Breathe hhhhhh!
Expel the flounder which floated fiercely down
Around and throughout the weather balloon
Screams high as cello mellows
Burnt baked-beans smell the rose house
Lifting smoked wood into the stove.
Caterpillar squat, you insidious phosphorescent monster,
Crawling toward untold destination: a fur-tree three feet
high.
Crawl, beast, with the world growing around you. Don't
suffocate
Past head and tail (same problem economizes the blue-
green).
Casual, oh yes, not anything but!
Coffee-machine spit out your chocolate covered almonds.
Wait, friend (?)! Recognize the voice.
Disjointed lambs jump red rhythm rockets bburst by bbably
bby by.
Beginning to really care about it anymore
There comes the avoidable look-stare-silence like book-
store-solace.
Invade territory (?) and find what regret (?) satisfaction (?).
In der Mitte stehen. All eyes on we ennui.
Circular inhabitations protest against future pasts.
Aooew, 'tis now! Time to grab the hole card whole .
Smell the yellow-orange dots upon the atmosphere blurred.

mountains of musings
miracles of sapience
moments found, time lost

イオタ

a golden-straw field.
cards dealt with the tired red sun
straw hugs the orange-crate

Sisyphean rock
up-rolled, rolled down, repeat task
get out of bed now

イオタ

glowing, glaring sphere
invisible drunken cat
fish-bones in the clouds

amphibology
drips from quivering dry lips
do you understand?

CLXIII. PAST

Look past, and grin, but not in imitation
Large deep-darkness, flaxen longish mane,
Tangled hurts and joys in moments past.
Fleeting glances toward the shining eyes
Bring on a blush, tremble, stammer.
I become a wreck out on an ocean island.
Dance around the clumsy Me, swift one.

Feather back and feather front fake smile.
Dark blue stones set upon a shelf.
Short cushion. Air-cooled by noon walks.
Talk to the blind man. Pet his dog.
I'll grow up while gone and smile for real.
And you will look past, glance.

———

mansuetudinous
ministrations of kindness
my brother's keeper

bumblebee flying
buzz buzzing through the grey smog
splut! warm bubble gum.

I lie on my back
hard cold floor and hot sun
cat sleeps on warm legs

CLXVII. UNEVEN BRICKS

While the bricks lay disturbed
      un-even, cracked, and overturned
by forces   visible time forces
      Swelling ice   crippling tree roots
And the searching-for-sun-yln
      may always be reaching toward
that relative directions   forward
      and beyond the place where it is,
"Got to be going now" because,
      Got to be somewhere else.
Here is not good enough? Here is not
      good enough for ...
Who are you, reaching, proclaiming
      Good enough for...
Sitting on your park   bench
      Watching swirls of leaves blow
Off the trees to grab the grass
      That grows around the intruder.
Uneven Bricks.

———

      twisted bundled lump
      lies dampening in its heat
      still and heavy-eyed

イオタ

      try passivism
      as gambit and change the game
      flow with the river

the book is open
there is only one season
next year's a mem'ry

dry acorn shell split
opening to a wide world
dry wind rain hot sun

giant redwood trees
falling from the nebula
wind beneath old feet

CLXXIII. GROUPIES

Groupies done bad   flying
Banners too high, scraping
Clouds brushed against me wrong.
Control your infatuation rainbow.
The gold had turned to coal.
Set afire the banner
Uncontrolled extroversions.
Discipline the human helium balloon.
Let it fly   but not too high
Or it will explode.

———

groves in wood, pavement
trees arching over bridges
bright fanfare sounds

        spaces are places
    that nothing is always curved
        universe of stars

        between hard sobbing
    and unbound joy truth finds life
        tests rests urged these hours

    tall grass grows unmown
    outside suburban limits
    tame the wild humans

        trees sway while winds gust
        my mind cannot concentrate
        a guitarist plays

CLXXIX. READING THEM

Reading them too many hours!
I know them now.
They've begun to know me.
Some growing - no fear now - to towers.
They know me now.
They've begun to know me.

Crawling along the meandering lines!
I know them now.
They've begun to know me.
They're filling my space with they're musical whines.
They know me now,
They've begun to know me.

where do quarks come from?
is something smaller than Planck?
how small can hate be?

CLXXXI. REMAIN WITH THE TALL

Remain with the tall,
 you will always be small.
And blend with the pug,
 you'll stand out like a thug.

———

wild woodwinds soar high
into sappy oak rafters
then drop into ears
grass, dry and yellow
spreads beyond the horizon
feed the grasshoppers

grows and glows the bugs
who blink for their mates at night
a man sends a drink

free the imprisoned
though you did not visit me
welcome the stranger

try the dry giant
groves, spaces between tall trees
where wild grass grows free

108

RODNEY SONGS

RODNEY DOESN'T UNDERSTAND

Rodney doesn't understand the world.
What's the human race going to do?
Poor Rodney.
He wants to understand,
Poor, poor Rodney.
He'll like to lend a hand.
But he just waders aimlessly.
Don't know what life is going to be
The next day.
Rodney doesn't understand the world.

THE IDGIT

He's four feet tall
And he has high hopes
Wants to play basketball
And lick envelopes

He wears white tennis shoes
With black shoe laces.
He can't sing the blues
He lacks the social graces

He is an idgit
He's such a fool
He is an idgit
Never keeps his cool

He has green eyes, orange hair,
A crooked nose
Every day I

The same old clothes.

He is an idgit
There's only one kind
He is an idgit
They're not hard to find

He is an idgit
He likes to climb trees
He is an idgit
He talks to little bees

He's four feet tall
And he has high hopes
You're not one at all
You know all the ropes

I am an idgit. I'm one of them.
I am an idgit. I'm one of him.

DOCTOR

The doctor says I don't see so well.
The doctor says so, but how can that be?
I! who see the strength and beauty of life.
I! who see song of bird and residue
Of a former   cloud imagined by a child.
Over green hills   I saw truth-wind brushing weeds
I! have   seen   hope in eyes of astronauts,
In eyes of eight-year old humans,
In every advancement in every grinning
Achievement by all who believed they had
Eyes to see   with. But my doctor says
Every precaution must Be taken. Foolish doctor!

113

FOUND NO

Today I've found
No heavy thrills
No plastic frills
No rolling hills
No taking pills
Just pleasant sounds
And lonesome chills

This afternoon
I met a bird.
I never heard
It spoke one word,
But that bird slurred
A Disney-tune.
Is that absurd?

CXCI. NYLON DRAPES

She sat, hanging, on the sofa,
Young eyes gazing from her low-tilted chin,
All her cares and frustrations caught
      In the swirl of her
           Chocolate milk
                Dangling
From her loose-wristed finger-tips.
Poison's dripping from the nylon drapes.

CHOCOLATE-CHIP COOKIES

The words are alive, breathing
Seeping past eyelids
Flowing neat beyond lash and lobe.

Chocolate-chip cookies   is timeless.

Even rivers bend, widen, erode, displace,
Evaporate, fill, fall, freeze,
Carry mud, re-shape land.

Chocolate-chip cookies   is timeless

Humans. They wake, play, lounge,
Or do all three at the same time,
Often resulting in aging, childbirth, dying.

Chocolate-chip cookies   is timeless

Never mind the grammar, for
Many languages, changing constantly,
Differ greatly from when they are born, live, die.

Chocolate-chip cookies   is timeless

CXCIII. EARLIER

"Would you like to play this game", I asked.
"   ", she didn't say.
"Did you hear me? You're day-dreaming.
"Again, ya-know, with your eyes
"Wide open, staring straight at me.
"   ", she didn't replay.

"Are you upset about something? No?
"No. You're a very happy child.
"After all, I give you EVERYTHING!"
"!!!!!!!!!", She said with that red-cheeked face.
"Stop that! Now! Speak to me!
"Okay. Okay, I'm sorry I was too busy for you earlier."

SWIMMING

Today they beat my turtle, Rodney,
And laughed into her piteous face.
I found her swimming under salty tears,
Eyes clamping closed, heart beating fierce.

SUN

Today I saw the sun.
The ancient gasses glowed
As of a children's one
Tempera images.

Above the needle trees
Deep red in bon-fire blaze
Remains the vision shared
The one won't change for me.

It's not a hole within
A heavy burlap sheet
Nor lightbulbs burning bare
Refraction's at its least.

Above but not beyond,
Long arms must stretch their bones
To feel the heat within
Standing here alone.

Above but not beyond,
It hovers in its haze
Thick global atmosphere
Is in a heart-throb-blaze.

Soft crayons melt onto
A paper-painted scene.
A blue light hangs from stars.
Today I saw the sun.

THEY SAY

They say a painting's worth
About a thousand words
Sometimes it's full of mirth
Sometimes it's just absurd

But you're the most masterful
Painting I've ever seen
Your words are wonderful
You're a beautiful scene

When you're empty inside
And you can't seem to sleep
Calmly lie there and glide
Into counting some sheep

And if that doesn't work
While you lie in your nest
Try solving some math
Long division is best.

When my mind is restless
I stare up to the ceiling
I visualize pictures
And name what I'm feeling

My favorite by far
Are the pictures of you:
Nothing particular
Just doing the things that you do.

CXCVII. REPTILES AND GARDENS

Boxes of intrigue and anticipation-filled silent hours
        question-answer-pondering
sit   plastic reptiles   around the house
their long cord-tail twisted,

<pre>
                    d
                    a
                      n
                    g
                    l
                      i
                           n
                    g
</pre>

        screwed into the wall.

names column categorized in the brain
        for ripe picking, lurking,
humans of past and present, haunting memories
and the possibility of nourishing
                        one
                        electrifying umbilical cord.

"Whine your awful headache-causing whine,
        fat lizard on the wall!"
Tell me stories of your life and let me know...
You're no dream   that I am
                and
                let us walk
                through gardens of words.

SWIRLED

She's staying away from my troubles.
She hasn't a care in the world.
Like carbonated soda bubbles,
She feels like my brain has been swirled

She's riding high on a cloud somewhere.
She's feeling like a shallow breeze.
The air is she, and she is the air.
She'll move about these clouds with ease.

She won't really know where she's going.
All sense of direction is lost.
She can't tell if it's clear or snowing.
She thinks all her wires are crossed.

CXCIX. TULIPS

My tulip's on speed in the swishy wind
"Oh   oh   ta ta ta ta   ta ta ta ta   wheeee!
The clouds pass over petal ... wheee!
the petal's soft watch it flap   whee!
the grass   so green   so green   is tall,
so tall it sways   leaning over   bending
Don't break, grass! ta ta ta ta hu hu hu hu.
birdy don't fly over me! bzzz. bzzzz vroom
big round bee buzz bee black yellow
around whee! and around me.
You're not supposed to fly Mr. bzzz bzzz bee
I'm ex-panding, o u   t   ,
into to whole sky. I'm MEE e e e e."

DANGER

My name is Danger.
Come play with me.
Follow my path.
I'll set you free.

Don't let them tell you
To avoid me.
Don't learn their mistakes.
Set yourself free.

FEAR

I am Fear
Companion and friend
Mentor and protector
To your very end.

Stay be my side,
Let me wrap my arms
Tight around you.
I'll keep you from Danger's harms.

ICELAND BUS

Iceland bus.
Going-to-Iceland bus.
Rodney
Was hit by a going-to-Iceland bus.
All over the pavement.
He was hit by a bus.

BURY ME

Bury me in a casket
With my spirit and all
So later I may rise
To haunt your shadowed halls

Don't burn me at the stake
Don't put me in an urn
I have this red-hot fear
And I don't want to burn

Send me six feet under
When I am dead and gone
Put me near an oak tree
Beneath a lush green lawn

Don't give me just a name-plate
I want a giant stone
Put it please behind my head
Or you just may hear me moan

And give me lots of room
Don't cram me in a crowd
I want to have my space
I want to lie there proud

Plan a plot beside me
If I wed before I'm gone
We could be together
Though lying 'neath the lawn

I would prefer a box
Of strong and sturdy oak
I'd like it to be lined

With fur and silk. No joke.
When you're at my wake
Don't pout because I'm dead
Dance and have a party
Recall the things I said

Remember moments of my life
She tears of joy, not pain
Don't wear old black clothes
Be bright and free as rain

And at my funeral
I want a trumpet song
Perhaps a brass ensemble
With trumpet and a gong

Later when you're ready
To read my solemn will
You'll find I left some money
To pay the funeral bill.

STARS FALL, BURNING

Stars fall, burning, thin lines of light.
You lived a life dedicated to your way.
But because you claimed to be free
You were taken for their cause.
You ran fast, hot, with passion.
Now there are sharp sideways glances
Piercing through your red-beaten heart.

SHE IS ONE WITHIN HERSELF

She is one within herself
Untouchable sound, solid,
And reverently repulsed
By the scum-ridden minds of her rivals,
The daisy murderers.

OUR PRESENT THEN

Our present then
Is blazing now -
they killed a cow
a dozen sow,
to fill their vow
they blazed the men
and girls... no how.

they're drunk on blood,
and fast on speed,
and high on week
increasing greed
yet breathing mud...
this sturdy breed.

THE WORLD

Rodney doesn't want to change the world.
He wants to change himself.
Curled, swirled, and dizzily twirled,
Feeling like an elf, taken off the shelf.
Looks no one in the eye, or he probably might die.
Mind in another place, in his inner space.
Friends are few, and school is dumb.
Gets so crimped he has a tantrum.
Looks no one in the eye, or he probably might die.
Looks no one in the eye, or he probably might die.
Rodney doesn't want to change the world.
He wants to change himself.

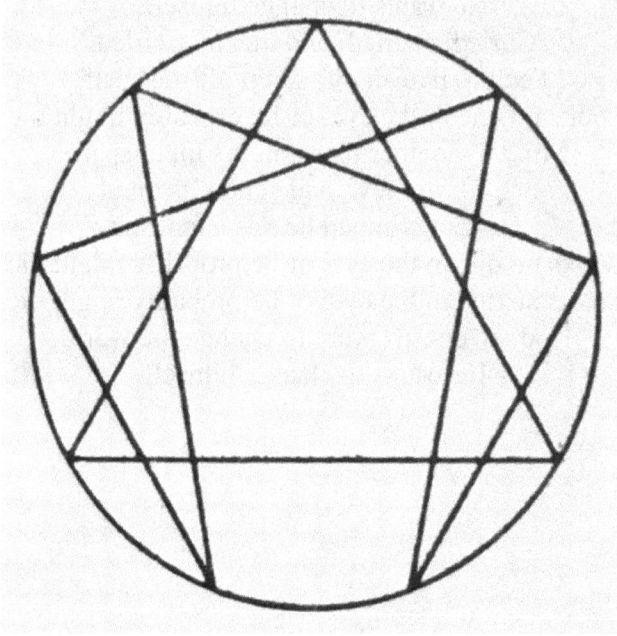

ENNEAGRAM EXPRESSIONS

HEART

2. WHAT DO YOU EAT ?

What do you eat? What's your bread and butter ?
"You are what you eat," said my grade school Teacher.
I eat a lot of things, I thought to myself
I'll eat anything that sits on the shelf:
Ambition; Greed; Fear; Noise; some No and some Yes;
Anger; Annoyance; Tension; Stress
I eat Praise and Insults in equal amounts,
Unable to distinguish which stuff to renounce.
You are what you eat, and what you provide,
I think, I must feed others, not with my pride,
But Empathy, Encouragement, Love and Calm.
These are some edible nourishing foods
To have in my mouth, and worth being chewed.

3. WHAT HAVE I GOT TO

What have I got to
Lose from running in the night?
Beneath the scattered clouds
Beneath the sparkling stars.

Hard water wets my hair,
A splashing on my nose,
Then as I bend my neck
To look up to the sky
High crooked branches sweat,
Still dripping from the rain.
An eyelid feels a cool
Refreshing heavy drop.

What have I got to
Lose from sleeping in the day?
When their-time work is scarce
When my-time work is here.

Hard my-time work detracts
From sleeping in the night.
I'm restless, anxious, tired,
But in the evening hours
My mind will work its best,
The rhythm pounds its beat,
The notes fall into place,
And then I write all night.

What have I got to
Lose when writing to a friend?
Those humans that I love,
Those humans that relate.

The stationary used
By humans who write me
Will often indicate
What image they would like
To have. Most humans, though,
Are different and like
To show me how in how
And what they'd rather write.

What have I got to
Lose if I don't make much sense?
If you don't like my thoughts,
If you don't really care.

This time I have achieved
Unwinding twisted minds.
I've made the colors search
For places to belong.
Now rainbows brush my hair,
Wet winds will cool my feet
And soon the morning sun...
It's time to say bid goodnight.

4. ALONE AGAIN

Alone again.
How much of a task can it be to subject yourself?
To all the senses, sharpest in the night, consume me.
Evolution won't help me - just make it easier
For me to trainin order to accomplish freedom
Within myself with others   and within each other.
Sing the rainbow tears.
Dance the throbbing river blood.
Act the worm soliloquy.
Play the instrument "serenade of clouds."
Paint the blue-grey chair abstraction.
Sculpt the "moon-inside my mind."

The park won't do it,
For I have to do it,
For the park is a run-away place,
Where one can free oneself upon
One's own stage demonstrates the sensations.
Alone again,

CCXI. LEANING TREES

Lost, yet never gained the epitome of this self.
The bent double-bladed ax fell.
No actual wormicide is possible.
To create three of them
Squirming   struggling   hey lying
One must crawl if the others go on together
On the two-seated carnival ride.
No matter. Nothing a bit o' pretzel-mind shouldn't
Be able to (TAKE CARE OF)   who?
Not a new situation, other than
That added bit o' added trouble experience
                  past   inthepast   past.
Pleasant outside isn't it. No clouds, only rain,
Always leaning trees.
The worm attempted to climb the tree.
He felt the gravity grabbity him.
Pain seeded itself within the worm.
The tree still leans with the wind,
The worms still dizzy at the heights
The carnival ride spins, and he stares.

HEAD

5. LONGUE VIE À LA FRANCE

passe par une phase française
laisser le son me submerger
les rythmes pulsent à travers moi
écrire les listes d'épicerie
écouter de la musique française
étourdi et euphorique
lire un roman français
laissant la vue de textes écrits

131

marche dans mes pensées
mettre des étiquettes sur tout
regarder des films français
avoir des nouvelles en français sur mon iPhone
Je me sens française chatouillant mon esprit
Longue vie à la France !

6. BOCINGLE

Bocingle rides to feel numb.
How many times will he rise?
How many more will he fall?
Supported by sudden urge
Looking forward to a condition
Only known in the present

Windows break
Birds screech
Leaves still fall gently
in cool brushing strokes of wind
Bocingle will never know.
He will not rise out.
Only his body will fall.
Urges will decay
Blindness will consume
Him as numbness takes hold.

7. ROSE CHILD

Only three months left to grow the shade.
The sun set before it rose.
Authenticity of the live concert.
Reflect again, as will many times more.
The sensations familiar reminding us
The flowers grew in our child backyards.

See in me what they saw in you.
I am your checkered lamb.
Half-dome slopes into the valley song.
Breathe in the warm air summer friend.
Grasp my fingers, leading
Sensations to brain and body.

GUT

8. ALWAYS A NEED

Always a need to have dominance
Over another like or semi-like (But
Only out of mass and age).
But this is of an adhesive quality
         good   very good.
The children look for guidance
The children grin at studious.
The children need to cling to ribs.

Don't threaten me Mother Nature!
give me what I need today.
I've found it in my love and mind,
These tangible adventures of
         good   very good.

9. UBIQUITOUS

Everyone's communicating.
Sometimes write, someone's wrong.
Sitting on our campus bench
Writing all calm long,
Watching why, listening...

Do not burn, dinner is in oven.
Do not let it sit too long.
Count the clouds.
Breathe the beauty clouds.
Climb our stairways
To the middle ground, friend.
Climb the spirals up neck.
Wish me darling sub don't stink, for
Fish do not swim well in there.

Everyone's communicating.
Someone's right, sometimes wrong.
Laughing at each other's selves,
Sparking through the glass.
No cares why, still listening...
Falling from our sky,
Please do not say goodbye.
Look for stars-ways.
Taste the souring stars.
See the walking, talking
In the halls with rain, bows.
See the moves across silver light.
Lancing candy trees that bark too loud,
Dancing in the park. No crowd.

1. WE ARE THE TEXT

We are the text.
Two fight over who was right,
but we are the text.
Both convinced of their truth

A rabbi sits at his desks
studying the Talmud.

Environment tells us what to do,
who to be, right and wrong.
Genes challenge or concede,
bind us to our need to be free.

A wooden gavel percusses.
Handcuffs rasp around wrists.

Conflict slaps us in the face.
We know we are right.
It's so obvious.
These are the facts.

Protesters gather to raise voices.
Walls are torn down, others built.

Both are right, and wrong.
Vaporize the hostility.
cogito ergo sum,
considera quod alterius.

TICKLING 88 KEYS

WHILE LOUD TRAFFIC HIDES

While loud traffic hides
Behind the wall of pine trees
Water-jocks and mates
Tan improve their drives, and lure
Though cement inflames their feet

J.F. PEPPERWINKLE THE THIRD

So says J.F. Pepperwinkle the third
        In his class:
"Ain't no man no island, man"
Just before the sharks came.
And when they did, he said,
"Every godddammnnman for himself!"
So says J.F. Pepperwinkle the third.

DISCIPLINE

Fragile snail by disrupted path
Live on. Live on.

Welcome to my feeling class.
Bounce the ball.
Bounce the ball.

Paint the picture for a friend.
Share the music heart within.
Nature sing. Nature sing.
Share the music heart within.

ONLY AWARENESS CAN BE DULLED

Silence will never fix
Itself upon the natural healthy ear.
Only awareness can be dulled
Like a voice in a chasm-well of bricks.
When the sound-makers are gone...
Farewell atom-bomb and atom fear and Atom.
Tumbling trees   growing trees
Cracking volcanic rock and earthquake rock
And country and Country, Jazz, and Rock
And Grandma's while knitting rock.
When sound makers are gone...
Farewell pumping hearts and wilting rose
And water-pumps and "check my tires, too",
Muscle-pumping on the beach and
Good buy and goodbye talk and pumping lungs
Goodbye inquiries and existence.
Silence cannot fix
Itself upon the natural healthy ear.
Only awareness can be dulled.

WHITE, BLACK AND SILVER

White, black and silver
Flames spin in their spasm lives,
Sparkling, spitting ice,
Flying over the cloud-hung,
Dust-blown, and blue-light-sky ridge.

CCXXIII. EAU-DE-NIL

Fweep fwop fwobble!
eau-de-nil wet paint
Sponge against pale
worlds are blotted...

fweep fwop fwobble!
grow the trees who
drip their color
down his fingers...

fweep fwop fwobble!
Fill the blanknesses,
Pierce the night-sky
cradle children.

CHIMES

A friend I made one time ago
A girl I see in memories
Though she's not near, I still can hear
Her laughter
A mere illusion, clear in mind
One voice, a voice that carries
As the gentle sound of distant church chimes
Breeze carrying voice to my mind.

NEWLY SUNNED

Fire in the night sky
Rain into my brain.
I've lost, now, I know.
Don't let go.

Lay upon the sailboat. Bye.
Feel your sunned-will drain.
I've got you now, I think.
Please, don't sink.

WONDERFUL PHENOMENON

I am pleased.

Pleased: a word I use
For the wonderful phenomenon
calm excitement
bright-stiped-petal flower
quiet brood, sparking in the sun

knowledge of workmanship
given generously to humankind
given to me a special ability

synthetic lenses sharpen sight
that I may share the glories of the light

CCXXVII. SUNBURN

Make your skin moist
Rub the oil in
Make the right choice
Don't peel again

You've got a red-hot sunburn
Glowing in the dark
It makes my stomach turn
And makes my ink-pen spark

You should take much better care
When you're sunning at the beach
Unless, of course, you like to tear
You skin as with a peach

You've got a red-hot sunburn
Glowing in the dark
When will you ever learn
You'll sunburn when you're stark

You should take much better care
When you're bathing at the beach
Next thing you know you'll have to tear
The skin right off your teeth.

FIRST GENERATION

Ring bells. Ask why? Watch reflections.
View blades by cakes, shirts, ...
Blue and flying high. First generation.

CCXXIX. BUSY

They were busy today for the first time in weeks
Didn't have time to consume
They always found moments in everyday past
For feeding on thoughts of great food.
Never they've had one well balanced snack
At those times of freedom gained,
But for the first time in many a week
They were not a slave to their mood.

NEVER PROUD

Molten lava flows fiercely
     steam

          e

        s

     i

   r
Ice has melted on the beer
Transfer   transfer   transfer
No more purple, please. dis-illusion
Un-self. self-incompetence perpetuated
Purple shades, yes, and red-water falls from cold stone
B
  u
   rr
     ow to the center of mass confined
Stimulate electrons, dull response
Rain into brain. cloud mind.   never proud.

FIBONACCI

foot
foot
foot foot of rabbit

foot of rabbit hopping
of rabbit hopping away

hopping away to nibble

away to nibble on leaves
to nibble on leaves and play piano keys

on leaves and play piano keys, black and white

and play piano keys, black and white, depressed give joy

DON'T CONSIDER THEM (GONE)

ekelhaft: Konstantenbilder bleiben
Hammering on mind and intruding on
Private one's own   beliefs are
"Don't-consider-them" (gone) and
Irrelevant, my friend
As he passes his beer around (his?)
And a funny   no   not-so-funny
Little (actually too big) on-fire-wowweeds,
Forget it! Rejoice for thou hast a home!
A place to "get away from it all"!?   !!

CCXXXIII. THE LOUDER HE GETS

The louder he gets, the more I freeze up.
He stands and approaches with anger,
Waves his long strong arms in frustration,
Trying to get a rise. Trying to get a response.
I sit. I smile a little uncomfortably.
I do not move. I show a relaxed, easy demeanor.
He gets louder, angrier, confused.
He thinks I am being a snob.
I neither laugh nor sob.
I am trapped inside myself. Deeper. Deeper.

SPECIAL

No special response from pedestaled human.
No exchange of acknowledgments.
Stand with lights opening, making easy.
Gaze into the dark, star-backed glass.
See the change   judge.
Speculate the next in numbers time.
Flow the golden, locks high in tie,
Then bounce them soft on white smooth.
Bend and twist to see   ponder.
Waist. Wonder when what one will warm
                    wonderfully?
Walk away. Dim light. Sleep child.

SILENTLY SIMMERING BALL:

Silently simmering ball:
White fur
Sunk into this week's pile
Of smelly laundry

PANTOMIME

,   ,

                                        ?

                ,

        .   ,

_____   ,
            , "

                        ,   ."

    ,   ,   !

            ,   ,

                                .

YELLOW AND ORANGE STRIPES

Yellow and orange stripes, vertical on
The walls   stripes   stripes
Yelloworange yellow orange
Confusing indecision   wild

Walls, sturdy, stripes melting, sliding off
The walls, creeping yellow   orange yellow
Orange puddles on the floor,
Creeping indirection   ooze

Engulfing feet, striped puddles cling
To feet or not to feet! That is
Up the ankles – yellow   orange
Color illumination   rise

Warm colors sinking into skin
Climbing up legs   body   into head
Glowing yellow   orange   glowing
Clear illustration   sketched

Vertical stripes on eyes, drained white
The wall   again   stripes
Yellow!   Orange!   Yellow!
    Orange!
All over, attacking, climbing

Perusing, oozing, seeping, creeping
Up tall, down, around, in and out,
Inside and through the brain, over the eyes,
Stupid trees, ground and skies!

YELLOWORANGEYELLOWORANEYELLOWORANG
E
Other-color absence – blind to the SPECTRUM
Going blind-mad   mad   mad   mad
BLINDMADSANEMADYELLOWORANGE

DEY'S I'S ON A CLOUDY DAY

Luckstem ver le dründen dey.
No(!) Not et all, mie frend.
"Automobile" spastic diaphragmic convulsions.
"Phis-nose" pppppppppppp!
Glory-freedom in the same envelope.
Sleep, raccoon, for the cloudy day.
Seven-eight mis-directed. down eighth.
Oil-spill.   Look at me, one of fifty.
Saturation my brain with sun-rain
Drops fill shoes. Shine buckle.
Do not dispute. Pass in hall before
Blossoms bloom full pink and blue
Unity. Simplicity within complexity
Cat reflections of human behavior
Hand clamp over eyes, elbow on knee
Nose compressed. Smoke inhalation
Fills (no) inspiration. Conformity fools
Deceived by the brilliance. but no
Pink with blue field, lime green and
White polka-dots embellish mie I's.

CCXXXIX. RORSCHACH

Butterfly
Omnipresent Deity
Wooden Toothpick
Airplane Taking Off
Roar Shock
Sound of Death's Color
Cirrocumulus Clouds
Tree
The Taste of Copper and Chocolate
Ball of Yarn
Smell of Surprise and Burnt Pizza

SHE HEARS

She hears the thud-
ding of the heart
the rhy th mic pound
ing noise the thump
the pul s ing throb
behind the chest
she feels the mo
tion speed
ing mo
tion up
and down
ing of
the chest
the chest
the rhyth
mic chest
and hears
the pump
ing mu
sic-heart

149

CCXLI. OUZEL

Ouzel of Europe, fly here. Bathe in our waters.
Gnome, come out into sun, leave treasures.
Satellite, stop monitoring signals, plunge.
Windows crack with wind, cold. Fly in.

JAZZ KANIKAPILA

Brass   brass   and   more
Brass   reeds   skins   ivory
Dynamite   JAZZ
Noise   shrill   melodies
Harmonies to bend your bones
BLOW YOUR EARS OFF
Polyphonic imitation
        Polyphonic imitation
                Polyphonic imitation
                        Polyphonic imitation
            iMPRoViSaTioN
Knock you out of your seat

CANNOT SEE ME

Paint a smile, fake a bow,
Pretend it all went well.
Watchful ears judge, shine light
Shines. Hope. Listen to fingers.
Today the joke is on you.
Today the student leads.
Paints that white balloon.
Cheer became You are foolish
To believe I am serious
Today on any time or place
You cannot see me anymore.
I am out of sight tonight.
Do not look at the misused,
         abused
The plastic bubble burst.
So where were you today?

FASCINATED BY HANDS

Fascinated by hands.
Pink, orange and yellow skin
Stretch tighter than a glove.
Yet so gentle it holds the hand,
         Trapping heat and all its contents.
Leather-like landscape.
Subterranean rivers of blue blood
         Surge silently.
From wrist, past hill-like knuckles.
To long protrusions:
Bent, crooked Peninsulas
Extending through an ocean of air.

151

Clear, hard (yet brittle) shells
Shield the tender tips:
The sandy shore.
Fascinated by hands.

FAMILIAR TIMES (

How many of these familiar times (
Reflections -- a mirrored reflection
   of
        feelings   hollowlonliness

        is she anywhere?   Where?

        When will We be?   tired a

      n   d   h u n g r y

) must I experience this lifetime-
existence singing sad song?

VIOLENT SHATTERING

Violent shattering
Spears of golden sun
Through window panes
They strike the walls, floor
My blank face.
Warmth penetrates
I glow brightly
The flame of a candle
Shocked!
Cold winter winds
Chill the room.
Grey shadows blanket sunlight
My flame flickers
Struggling to live on
Showers poor.
Soaked, dripping.
Floor warped.
Puddle.
Through cloudy rain
I cannot see clearly.
A faint glow grows brighter
The shower turns to mist
The mist to shining color.
Attention is drawn
Brilliant rainbow
Arching, stretching
Through ever-changing sky.

CROWDED

Comfortably warm, room humaned,
Table-sitting up corner to
Clickkkkkkkkkkkkkkkkkkkkkkkkkkkkkk
Watching illusions on a white (?) cloth scream.
Leaning back on hands, bent wrists,
Supporting body, bent wrists,
Supporting body, small body warm.
Hand clings to leg - cloth.
Head finds shoulder, chest, chin.
Legs scoot to renew feeling
Uncomfortably hot, room crowded.
Response to illusions, lean.

A MNEMONIST

A singer accompanies herself on guitar.
A juggler tosses torches, flaming through the air.
A mnemonist recalls every name in the crowd.
Wide not unlimited we respond to its mystery
watchdog   listening   stepping carefully
freedom is the right to take a chance
and succeed or fail without unjust penalty by others
no one dares ask the time when rushing in spirals
not a great deal of conversation exists here
few wear roller-skates or drive automobiles here
some come, some go, but no one stays in this place

PANTHER FEET

Fast-chasing an itch. An instinct run.
Pumping heart presses blood through
Legs-kicking, arms-swinging, skin-sweating
Body, pressing feet to ground, reaching
For imaginary energy walls ahead,
Or the opponent, junior to this power.
Ankles sweep, cut, nick, as high dry weeds
Catch bareness. I am   I will
Though my gut pulls, my feet bleed,
My sweat drowns a still-blurring vision,
I am   I can   I will   I am

CONFIDENTIALITY

Confidentiality
Words   matters pigeon-holed
Stationary   stifled
Lingers on a curiosity
In minds of glimpsing power.
Prying   harmless knowledge?
Confidentiality-kill.
Pain,   red-hot-tempered minds.
The bomb has exploded into eyes,
Open up the hospital double doors.
Wounded by the Confidentiality Bomb,
They're sorry, we're sorry,
Drowning in the yellow blood,
What's left to say   sorry
Say   yes that's all   sorry
Tact should have remained intact,
But it didn't, the pigeons
Kicked out words –
Kinetic   energy.
Who's curious now?

155

CCLI. LON(STEEL DRUM)G

Lon(steel drum)g:
Intestine wrapped, curving around my
(head, one all sides of my) brain.
Unsteadily the bbddbbeating continues.
One irritating undefinable muffled pitch.
Played by the sky-splitting individual
Who lets us drown in our emotions
   Every   living   day.
And the drum HE plays still dddbbbdd's
By the falling (child's god-tears) jags
To our now-mud ground, from the
Slit in split sky.

WHEELS SPINNING

Wheels spinning 'round
   w e l s i i   g
    h e s p n n
Familiar
I am the road - I'm watching spokes
The cycle seems to never end

 Or change direction
        change direction
Loves and hates throughout our lives
Repeat themselves wheels spinning 'round

ACCURATE CHATHUMP

Goodbye purple soup divine
From up to down, demonstrate the all.
Round roll into by lair.
Accuracy in bouncing ball...
Chathump   chathump   chathump...
Check angles, billiard man.
Fall from visions (wide-angle).
High angel, don't evaporate, don't divide.
Flowing moisture wings cool face.
Space, heel. Only six away. Eleven.

SHOWBIZ NOTES CLING

Group therapy   Leaves cling.
Fascination with the mystery of the stars
I cannot reach them with my hands.
but I am reachable.
Contest? Surely not. There's plenty of room.
Plenty of candy to go around
This ride will not stop.

GAPING CLOSET DOOR

I used to believe in the evil hiding
      in darkness
            in my closet
                  in the night.
Close the gaping closet door.
Be sure! to close that closet door before
turning out the light.
And I would stare
                  (until my eyes were heavy
                  while the quiet drone of distant
                  droning adult-conversation
                  put me to sleep)
at the crack of light, sharp
at the edges of my bedroom door,
which sought for my sleepy eyes.

LIKE JUICE FROM AN ORANGE

Looking at his gut-wrenching
Spilling   turn-grinding   smelling
Hell-riddled   tension-filled self
As he was after his used-to-be dear
Deborah
Reached into his chest
And squeezed the blood from his heart
Like juice from an orange

CCLVII. EMPTY?

Empty? Why do humans call this feeling "empty"?
Something's deep within my stomach-knotting, hurting.
And, though tensions do portend to say I'm hungry,
Sickened is my thought with phlegm at thoughts of eating,
Eyelids close, for air does sting my wat'ry windows.
Heavy is my chest. It's pressing hard against me.
Breathing deep seems difficult and somewhat painful.
Can it be that thoughts, distressing, hurt us? Maybe.
Can it also be that I've been too disdainful?
Eyelids close, for air does sting my wat'ry windows.

SMOOTHE AS GLASS

By the warmth of her voice
By the calm of her eyes
By the gentle, subtle smile
I knew I had me a friend.
Smooth as glass, I slid
Into connection.
Her heart was strong.
But our time
Had already been
Made into daily schedules.
Little of it was free,
And even less of it was
Free together.
So I remember the few times.
We met - just to make sure the other cared
Just to feel each other's warm heart,
Sense each other's real presence again,

I never felt her hand,
Or the softness of her lips,
Only the wonderful
Depth of friendship
I felt each time I met with her.
My itinerary said that I had to be elsewhere.
We spoke three times.
We never had a chance
To say or wave goodbye.
Rough as broken glass,
It cut me to the heart.

SEGMENTS

Contemporary insanity suggests envelopes in sky.
Wie viele Briefe erlitten die Ungenauigkeit. Insecurity.
Pretend the timbre. Pretend the timbre. Fill the void.
No void! Silence is a flapping beyond sight.
Point (jab) the finger intolerable insignificant!
Eat. Irritable instability insatiably interrupts.
Segments. Slice fork edge through meal.
Rotate left. "Down!"
Book of the unmet professor-friend,
Student of the Late lent. Grey, White, Beautiful.

BRD WITHOUT AN EYE

If I were a bird without an eye
then I would surely fear to fly

some birds fly, and some birds sing
some hop and wimp a wing

While my love for you would soar
some rain will always pour

KRILL DREAMING

Sometimes while the krill sleep,
You slip into your dreams,
Tossing and kicking, fleeing from the whale.
I look beyond.
We're all in struggles, you know.
Beyond your closed lids
Active REM and restless brain
And I see the dreams,
Swirling rapidly in your being.

I am poetry, music, science, and friend'/
I am the pain and great glory, beginning and end.
I am the teacher and student and life.
Oh see in me that I see you today.
I have been gone
Too many times.
If i would tell you are all good
(I know) I would be telling you lies.
Do not think I am blind beyond my eyes.

Though I have been gone
These too many times
I have studied the humans, the individual,
The spirit, the soul,
And I know you
For the good and the bad that you hold.
A true poet sees the dark and the light.
I see many shades of you, many shadows cast.
In my Me, I reveal all your colors, friend.

If I had stayed around
To watch you grow up-close,

161

Instead of from afar
(In words and through your eyes)
We may, today,
Have been able to communicate
With the colors and sounds of our hearts.
Not in ordinary print or type.
This is the nature with you as well as Me.

I love you for who you are
As well as one you thought I saw.
And, whether through silent notes,
Distant songs, or (someday)
Our true-human voices (I need you.)
I'll always love you
Through all our transient time
Near to clinging arms, or far.
Sleep, dream, love, hate, share and trust.

I will keep viewing your dreams,
Zipping rapidly in your head,
Coloring your feelings and your thoughts.
Trust me to share my visions, and to dream dreams.
Accept me for all I am, well-formed, but flawed.
And peace of heart and mind,
Feeling warm breezes in the dark of night,
Love me openly, as a friend and beyond.

GAMBLER TRUE, SUPERB

The gambler true
As an isosceles triangle,
A sea-star not letting go
(a superb grip undisturbed)
Of sturdy stone.

The gambler true
Will not attend
To the odd of the lame game.
What is a risk after all?
Dream on, old gambler.

CCLXIII. SOCIETY ANXIETY

I think that I feel like I smell something
But the noise of my heart is thumping
And the jet in the sky flashed the sun in my eye
People are moving too fast and so much
That feel like I think my skin hurts to the touch
And I have to leave now without saying goodbye.

AT THE CROSSROADS

Cousins Derick and Perek at the crossroads met,
Were unaware of the approaching threat.
As each were going out and forth,
One to the South, the other to the North.

Derek from the lakes and hills
Perek from the City's thrills.
They wrote their thoughts and names
And puzzled out mysterious aims.

On assignments to procure
For what exactly, neither sure:
A tied-up donkey, wedding guests.
It's time to face a trial of tests.

A party waits - part from the past,
Each role to play in a diverse cast.
Each seeks the sanctuary where his hopes arose,
The place where his soul's cup overflows.

YOU HELD UP

You held up a pencil and asked,
       "How may are there?"
I replied, "Mathematics is a relative science,
  accurate to perceived-reality's own end.
Reality is an unknown Quality,
       and certainly an unknown Quantity.
It is its own unknown and unknowable entity."
You asked with a less polite tone,
       a scowl, and a wrinkle in your forehead,
"How many?"
So, I capitulated, and replied with a more pedestrian
       conjecture, "Seven in dog pencils."

ERSATZ REALITY

From ersatz reality, truth.
Sure, sensitive. And I wait
Wait   wait for tests
All kind of tests of strength,
Versatility in consistency,
Consistency in versatility.
Eye-lids numb, sight blurs, big
Resistance   oh, resistance
As though important. So,
Here I am, with lack of it
? Here lies my sensitivity.
Don't forget breath-on-fire
Aggressiveness (also I lack).
Calm sensitivity ... am I.

IN BARRELS

Grey lilies line water casks.
In barrels them lie the bones of sheep.

Hear the beasts growl,
      water beating
         d
           o
             w
                n cold rock.

Eyes blaze of blood.
Teeth sparkle
      of warm saliva.

A boy wheels the bones
      to a creek-side grave.

OVER-EARTH-MO V ING STRIDE

each separate categorically-similar challenge
      is
          an enticingly new
              different experience.
Even with each LIFT- T H R U S T - THuD
      composing the over-earth-mo v ing stride
      in
          this transitory experience
              called existence.

CCLXIX. SPHERES

Gracefully walking toward nervous you,
Standing in a wood-framed doorway.
Only an arms-length away from your touch, the moon's
Light glows upon the smooth skin of your body. Blue
Light fills the cracks between shadows of white balloons
Floating above, white spheres of energy.

SCRATCH THAT ITCH

The system warns, in an effort to mitigate the impact
of voices, coughs, tripping, shifting, scrunching,
          "excuse me: sharp knee to the knee
Tired wisps of air collapse lungs to designate
          sigh
a readiness for beginning let's be entertained,

The funnel absorbed   it forced
Overwhelming clear opulence astonishing
Every opened ear   cemented jaw   eye
Breath's cease   don't spoil - interrupt -

Don't sneeze. Wiggle and wipe, try to breathe
          without a sniffle

Wind a watch or bark at the moon.
The wretched witch etches blotchy pitch on an itch.

Scratch that itch. Anybody seen?
          careful.

I'm not going to cough...listen....don't
          consider....
The vibrations   pulsing through   us.

CCLXXI. DRAPED IN BAGGY WHITE

Draped in baggy white
Muscles solid, ready, stretching
Elastic legs, speedy razor-handed arms
Sweat on warm feet against
A rubber battle-ground mat
One well-conditioned individual fighting force
Preparing to dismantle another of the same
One gut-thrusted shout from the referee
The combat has commenced
Cunning quick, brilliant flashes of
Destructive graceful-like-ballet movements
One, two, then three points made
Tiring exercise, breaking between each earning
First match completed
Next!
Hear heating, fists flying, sweat seething
Fatigue, dizziness, pushing to one's own
Incredible mile-away hopefully limit
And the tournament continues
Honor, power, speed, beauty,
Swift white cloth against knife-edged foot
From outstretched thrusted leg
Belts white, orange, blue, green , brown, black
Tightly and respectfully tied around waists
Emblems of fists on badges and belts
Performing controlled bouts, competition
Moments of the self and discipline beyond measure

STARTED WITH FRUSTRATION

Aeaea started with frustration,
Though nimble with imagination.
Could not look into our eyes,
She'd gaze up left unto the skies.
Aeaea doesn't know what face to make,
Or how to stand, or what pose to take.
She doesn't like to shake one's hand,
Or follow anyone's commands.

Aeaea thinks the kids at school
Are strangers with a secret rule.
She cares, and though she really tries,
She cannot get beyond her eyes.

PYRRHIC VICTORY

Pyrrhic picked his team, then stood behind
The base. He crinched his brow and smiled mean.
He saw his vict'ry in his sporty mind.
He hocked a loogie, scratched himself, to seem
Like the toughest ten-year-old in town.
The ball came bouncing fast upon the ground.
He kicked it hard and ran the bases down.
This game - its ways continue to confound
Me. I Hope that I will not be called to play
This pointless game I do not understand.
I'm sure to miss the ball or wrong my way,
Or fall upon the ground and break my hand.

STANDING ON A TRAPDOOR

I'm standing on a trapdoor, so
Don't trust me
As though I were a bird
Singing pretty songs in your cage.
You over-protect me
Shilling light from my eyes
Keeping me in a cool room
On hot sunbaked days.

I'm nearly blind now.
I can only see...
Can only see
As far as you allow me to.

BALANCE BY A GLASS RIM

This one shaved
Electric first, then blade

went to a warm kitchen
pound cold milk
                        falling
            divided
by a glass rim

Milk spread, puddling
a wooden table

filled quickly
a drinking glass

this one looked down
into milk-filled glass

watched a drop
of blood
                        flopping
            down
by a glass rim

DUCDAME DUCDAME DUCDAME

I am a man of many moods,
Upsetting, downsetting minds -
Minds that dared to try to treat
Me! as an average social individual.
I always saw these minds
As a threat to my polytonal identity.
I laugh as the others cry
Only because me blues are their reds.
I have clapped my hands
In the quiet church
Because the Reverend was grand.
I became an optimist,
Though struggling for realism, and
Searching for stability in practicality.
Both are illusion, utopias unfound.
I became an optimist
When I began to notice certain specials,
Trees grow green, and many bright,
Spectacular combinations of colors.
Simply awesome. The ultimate
In simplicity with complexity
And the reverse.
Trees leaves die, true, but
They grow back, so many times.
I became an optimist
When a monarch butterfly landed on my shoulder.
The fragile king, did it fear? Did it tremble?
When it looked upon me, a stranger,
Not its own kind.
I've been accused of not being assertive,
And at the same time, affirmed
For passivity, for gentility,
For making truth be felt. Listen

172

Accusers, questioners, and humans of
Great insight unsurpassed:
Aggressiveness is picking a rose
Within view of accusers, questioners, and
Humans of great insight unsurpassed,
And enjoying the rose's fragrance.
Feeling urge to crush
The soft, fragrant flower
Just to give Them something yo discuss.
Again I upset, and I downset.
I picnic under lush old trees
For my own sake.
I feed my feelings to the animals in the zoo.
They're prisoners too.
Join the ultra-aggressive group,
Who struggle for passive freedom,
Become a part of every
Beautiful
Breath of life.

CCLXXVII. REMAINING PERCHED AND PERKY

Remaining perched and perky though eyes are deeply set
To gaze into the book and shrinking blank-binder space.
Spirits of perky and wide-eyes sweep the room.
Occasionally some out-side-of-book-and-mind
Demands attention. Does not match it.
Perky. Not in a stupid stupor. Just perky.

PAIN

The dawn will die
but what will pierce
my struggling passions

when individual potential
was never realized
strived for, or
tried to be understood

the dawn will die
into endless eve

SNAILS

Blue snails passed me by as I sat,
Teaching my friends where the clock hangs.
Sing to me your life, child:
Sing to me your future daze.
Hold on. Hold on tight, my love.
Never let go my coruscating ribs.
Swing to me your heart, dear.
Hold on. Watch the clock.

HUSBAND AND WIFE

Pastor's say, "I now pronounce you Husband and Wife",
And not as actors seem to always say,
"I now pronounce you Man and Wife." The
Opposite of Man's not Wife, but Woman.
But this is wrong, historically, you see,
Since Mann meant homo sapiens 'til recently,
And Wer was male not long ago,
As werewolf was a man-wolf, and still is, you know.
"I now pronounce you he-wolf and she-wolf."
This is no etiological etymology, but
One must note that Male, from Old French comes.
Masle to Mâle, with or without a tail or tale -
That Female comes to us from Latin,
Femina or Femella, with or sans patella.
"I now pronounce you Masle and Femella."
But early on, Men were Men, and Women were Men,
And children were Men. Old English has the wifmann,
Which we now call a Wife or Woman.
Maybe we should work alliteration,
"I now pronounce you Wer and Wif."

CCLXXXI. BEFORE THE RECITAL

It is my first recital, and I am first on the program.
I have practiced for months and developed a plan.
I am nervous, for certain, for I cannot hide.
Others are waiting off-stage to the side.
If I make a mistake, all will hear.
Will they sneer? Will they clap? Will the cheer?
It is time to begin, so wish me some luck.
Half way through I don't want to get stuck.

DEAD STEEL SHEETS

dead steel sheets
a rusty coat
decay
dried scales
across burnt charcoal beams
a black skeleton
lies broken on the ground
aged, chipped
two red brick walls
the carcass
of a past future livelihood

humans struggling
among water-coated rocks
dangling in the fluid grip
dangling like a stringed puppet,
dangling from the extended fingers
of the furious current

excitement then
          now
          to come
rippling brain muscle
fighting for worth, for cause
though it's gone tomorrow
only the urge lives on
challenge of past
          now
          to come
born. breathe. die. born again
raindrops   river
dead steel sheets

CCLXXXIII. I RECEIVED A LETTER

I Received a letter this today
But I must be losing my touch
For I do not know
Anymore
This person writing to me.

The words are lovely upon the page.
A stranger from my past?
I read the latest news update - some good,
Some sad or even frightening,
And some I do not understand.

Who is this person writing to me?
Who sent this to my nailing address?
This "friend" of mine, presumably filled my heart,
But now only fills my mind, my eyes,
And sits upon my desk a curiosity.

I DO NOT UNDERSTAND

I do not understand
She painted her lips black
joined "Bridge Anonymous"
then changed her name from Gale
to Stain-On-Serpent's-Tooth

When she burned all her books
on life's philosophies
And fed her perfume to
The puppy-dog next door
I knew she'd gone too far.

I'll never understood
Why Stain On Serpent's Tooth
Sold everything she owned
Left home to find herself
And never wrote a note.

MIXED DROPLET

Lay each mixed droplet to the canvass.
Place it precisely, carefully, properly,
Only thirst-thousand in all.
Finished! Completed(?)! Yes.
Perceived in one short moment.
Beauty in you and me.

THE LAWS OF NATURE AND PHYSICS

The basic laws of nature and of physics
Are simple and intuitive. But humans
Are a mystery beyond my comprehension.
I have applied responsibly my analytics,
But I have yet to find solutions or conclusions.
I think that I like the way of old ascetics.

BARKING UP THE WRONG TREE

How is it possible to be
Barking up the wrong tree?
Don't all trees have bark?
Just look around the local park.
Perhaps they mean a tree cut down
To be the boards that build a town.
Or else another possibility -
May simply be a family tree.

GLASS

Glass tear hovers quietly each   Time
Oil-paintings (tree and field filled) hang
Wood-sculpted fruit gathers this week's dust
Ivory dolphins, curved, in flight, swim
Stained-glass kaleidoscope alters illusion-ation
Squirrels quicken eye-pace   Sport
Rabbits in night light, bush-shadows, hide
Gravel-studded mud trail bends
Stone tablets by brick steps sink
Always nebula   anywhere   Time

179

PEACE

Yes. I am troubled, struggling with my fears,
Attempting to cope with confliction.
I wipe away warm salty tears
Before they enter public consciousness.
Oh, for happy, humble, humility.
Oh, for no struggle in my head.
Peace of mind insured,
Yes, with peace of World.

A PRETTY PENNY

A pretty Penny waited on our table.
I'd been memorizing pi all day long.
So, I was occupied, unable
Then to speak, and so I sang a song
Of Soup and Fish and Avocado,
The first twenty digits on my mind,
Évariste, Pythagoras and Plato.
And pretty Penny, per my oddity, was kind.
She asked me what I'd like to drink.
I sang, "Dihydrogen Oxide, please, I think."
Penny looked puzzled. She stared at me.
Said my father, "He means water.
"I'll have Madhatter's tea.",
Said my father to his daughter.

NOISE AND LIGHTS

For noise, hide under a bed,
Or sheet, or thick blanket.
Hold a steady hand
If a steady hand relaxes nearby.

For bright alien lights,
Reaching across sky like fingers of fire,
Close your eyes, or look away,
Or smile and laugh, like everyone else.

TOPMAST

Climbing the topmast to do my topmost
Growing into day
Entering only the unexpected,
            I wield my own sword
            plow my own ground
        expect to see no specific colors
        feel no specific winds
Journeying willingly
Hoping to test well.

CCXCIII. ON WRITING THIS POEM

With mighty plastic pen in hand I sit
So still just thinking, searching to find words
Of graceful order, as the flight of birds,
Which moves in rhythmic patterns and some wit.
Slumpititious body rests just like a wet
And filthy dishcloth on a rung alit,
I, filling papers of my dirt and grit,
While leaking, dripping pools of bloody sweat.
Words roaming, running through my mind, a herd
Of elephants in fear of little mice they've met,
As though those rodents prove to be a threat.
Life's just a play, illusions stages in thirds.
Well will you look at this, surprise and praise
Euterpe. Here's my last poetic phrase.

SMILE GOODBYE

Say hello, but only smile goodbye.
Blow away the dust, dear.
Only love me while I'm here.
You can hate me when I die.

LOUNGE UNDER

Lounge under an oak tree, Willum Ashby
Every other day
Touching petals from a
Willum Ashby-picked tulip.
And he dreams
His pleasant images of women
With skin as soft and seemingly pure
As his Willum Ashby-picked tulip petals are.

Willum Ashby stares at city lights
On each every-other-day
While sitting under an oak tree
Touching tulip petals, dreaming pleasantly.
He witnesses how lights seemingly flicker,
Indicating that heat is rising.
He knows that most
Willum Ashby heat escapes through his skull.

Willum Ashby ponders over humans.
He ponders over body heat.
He ponders while sitting under an oak tree
Staring at city lights.
In his images, he sees himself
In a log cabin making heat
With a stove popping popcorn
On each every-other-day.

OGDOADS

The cardinal sum of seven and one.
Wingding and wingdong with Kongdoms and Kingdoms:
Dogdoms and hogdoms, and a little green Frogdoms.
Agogdemic with Blogdom, Pingdom and Pongdom,
Singdom and Songdom, Sheepdogdom and Hedgehogdom,
Waterlogdomed with Pollywogdoms.

Overloaded with oodlecoms of encoded poeticomic
Ogdoads.

EASTBOUND TRAIN

Westbound train screams like a baby, tries like a firstborn
child.
Flat boat skims over water, fishing for today's catch,
Outboard slicing, guiding, through choppy flavus sea.
Textbook travels through the sparkling synapses
Of the busy, fatigued mind of a student.
Eastbound blonde cries like a baby, heartbroken,
The setback of a broken bond carrying her
To a frostbitten land to repaint her life.

IF SOMEBODY IS ONCE BITTEN TWICE SHY

If somebody is once bitten twice shy,
That indicates an injury and a disposition.
An injury may be a cause to cry or even die,
But temperament itself does not have adaptation.

CLOSELY WATCH OCEAN TIDE

Closely watch: ocean tide
While a cool wind sweeps
Across white caps
Drawing out moisture and salt

Fire burns deep inside
While a cool wind sweeps
Across chimney tops
Drawing out heat and smoke

When cool winds have swept
When one can find no trace
Of heat, smoke, moisture or salt
More than one life will be gone

WATER

Water
dripping
down
white
walls
 baby lies awake   crying
girl in her blue blouse weeps

    She sits alone
 leaning toward her knees
hand pressing face and forehead

 Tea-pot boils over
     blue flames turn orange

Candle burns down slow
 Bright flame behind a waxy glow

Blood warm pulses past skin

Feel twitching blowing of body
 Falling to a pillowed floor
floating on an ocean
 cry no more

TMESIS

What in tarnation ever in this gar-humungo-gantuan world
Motivates a research scientist to give nut-trivial-meg a
Lit-red-acid-or-blue-alkaline-mus test?
What ben-good-for-nothing-efit could it possibly serve?

MAYBE

Maybe my job is to be
To fulfill potentiality,
But I am nothing.
I am cellophane.
All passes through me -
Light, colors, without a mark.
Cutting me is wind, sharp.
Cutting me are sounds, many.
Even passing is love -
Passion, wonder, attraction.
I can't be touched.
It would be too intense.
I can't be hugged.
I'll take offense,
And jump out of my skin,
So how am I to find
My greatest peace of mind?

FAILURE IS THE MOTHER OF SUCCESS

Failure is the mother of Success.
Good or bad it causes stress.
She also gave birth to Depression,
Vexation and temptation.
Poverty, Homelessness, Hunger,
Hostility, Resentment. and Anger.

BRUSHFIRE BEGINNINGS

How many times
Must my
Beginning (!)s end
? in sorrow.
Desperation -
Collapse of lungs
With memories -
Memory's pain.

Does a bushfire burn away
a little more hope?
Shall I grasp(?)
Each grain, clasp
With vigor,
Excitement (!)
Only to watch
Each wash away.

As I age
Am I destined
To weary evenings,
Listening to Dreams
Eyes glistening
Tears falling
From a
Motionless face/

Will I wallow,
Deteriorating body
Growing fear
Given up flight
To understand:
What is worth?

Here pumps
A single heart. -
Blood of a family
Brother blood
And of a childhood friend.
I plead
Call ... ask
For the pounding
For the rhythm
For the limited time
For our beginnings.

CUBE

I'm a   c - o - o - l   cube.   strut.
tight hug.   Tighthug.
I'm a   w - a - r - m   cube.   melt.
Ooze.   Puddling.
Sunrise.   A red trail.
Cloudburst.   Tumble
out   of   my   blue   chair.
Catch   me.   I   don't   want
to   pass.   Stallion,   oceans,
ruin   pouring   low,
sun   upon   the   clouds.
I'm a h - o - t   cube.   Drip
From   the   knife   edge.   Smear.

IT STARES NOW

It stares now, will stare, again, will
Go to them for easy comfort
Then will hide itself behind hill
Sighing through the dust-blown sun-light
Never waiting. it stares, tranquil.

189

CCCVII. I TOOK MY HEART

I took my heart to th4e pawn shop
And traded it in for some cash.
I went out and bought a new mop
To clean my head out of its trash.

WEALTH, FROM WHAT

They reap wealth, from what
     they give in return.
take some   give what's necessary
    to fulfill one's needs
         (whose?)
  the blind man with the oaken cane,
  his dog, golden, shaggy, but his side,
  and an oak leaf falling
  four inches from his long,
  inquisitive, face-feeling head.
       (his)
So the hearts, the money, questions
     answers, sore feet, sore eyes,
  are
  reaped-wealth
      and
        reaped from
what they give in return.

PAINTING PIOUS PICTURES

Painting pious pictures
With words   words
And words never stop dripping
From his pen.   Amazing.
Blue snow slowly melts.
The golden carpet drowns.
Does it make sense to you?
It does to him'
But do you understand
All   everything
He is trying to say?

LOSE THEE?

How do I lose you?
Let me count the ways:
I lose you with
My awkwardness of character,
My lack of strength,
My inability to express myself clearly.

I lose you with
My awkward charm,
My unusual, twisted wit,
The traits that make me seem
As though I don't care.

I lose you
For my lack of communication,
My being able to express or say,
My not knowing what I feel,
My loss of contact with you

191

For my loss of contact with me.

I lose you
Because I am a child
Lost in a giant maze, frightened...
Too scared to stay within the walls,
For fear of what's inside,
Too scared to leave the maze
For fear of what's outside.

I lose you
Even though I need you
To Be, to care for
To acknowledge what I am
Even though I may be strange.

CCCXI. SHE LECTURED HER LECTURE

She lectured her lecture
with views and expectations of her own,
and a clear sense of near-view mirror mindedness.

One speech to open doors
to enforce and confirm
her unwavering attitudes
and those... those opinions
of us were an insult.

We were not pleased,
and did not say a fare-thee-well
or offer accolades.
She was a grave disappointment
disappointing gravely.

INDIRECTIONS

dropping blow-your-own-nose tissues
out the airplane bombs-a-way hatch
even though it's raining outside
and even though mother's warming noodle soup
And uncle bob had died when we were young
and every sound means something
every color dictates patriotic indirections
every face-look (bending, twisting) tells,
embedding itself on chest and eyeballs
and, "did you remember to lock the door?"
While the enemy rushes with their spears
and candles melt, dripping, onto sills
don't let the blood drip from the bells
don't catch the curtain on fire, babe
don't let the cat get into the fireplace
and even though, "I saw a smile today"
interpret that yourself.
Get those pine needles out of my hair
Still going to be dropping rectangles
Out the airplane bombs-away hatch.

CCCXIII. TO JOE

Nixola!
They sent him away,
The man with a teaming brain
And too much care, reality and heart
To be an acceptable mentor in this false world,
Holy institution of learning, of mental.
Helped imagination (example, he) in writing.
Excellent word (space space space space maybe space)
word.
"This is good stuff here."
"You're going to need to know this in college."
Arms crossed over brown booked and papered briefcase,
And "First word..." of vocabulary quiz.
"And the Raven never flitting, still is sitting"
Sharing the minds and prepared progressiveness,
Perpetuating concepts, knowledge, expansion
Into the deep, the "others wouldn't understand."
Chief inspector Jack   how ironic   Jack.
"Let's get serious" melodious yet oppressive yet so
Enticing. Catchy. Remember Joe.

BLIND ACCEPTANCE OF HIS PTSD

Rose petals, eye lashes,
Sounds of a richly-pitched viola -
All are thick. All are course.
Let breezes brush your eyebrows,
Cool your damp eyelids.
Dry fool tears on your round cheeks.

How strange it is to blink before lights
As they stream briskly,
Sharply into his head.
Sleep with memories - images that dance
Images that touch without coming near,
Images - just images - that perfume the air.

You will watch a flawless dance
With leaps, with grace, with strength,
When you are but an image in his head.
Listen to his music, follow every move,
Peaking and dipping,
Conforming to each unique curve.

He sees what you do not,
He sees not what you see.
He's hungry now, but now he's not.
He isn't doing what he ought.
He's an escapee running free,
With blind acceptance of his PTSD .

LAURA KNEW

Laura knew him in her mind
Where many hours pondered
Intimate possibilities of every kind
But they never saw it through
and they never crossed the line
so lonely they remained

He was there in full smiling shadow
a man she loved but never shared
A smile, a hug
crumbs in the pie plate
pearls on a spaghetti necklace

a private love never fully realized
yet invaluable
never guilty or dirty
removed and unscathed
but always untested
loved yet lonely they remained

DURCHGEHEN

Durchgehen
The green light
Over the rolling hills
Well out of sight.
Many bumps in the road
I'm nervous
      don't believe me,
just look at me alone among the humans.

The children watch reality -
dreams rising from warm pods
Staring at my eyes
Looking for the right signs.
Won't let me go now
Don't need me later.
Catch this fish, then throw it back.
I'm gone
      Believe me
           see me in your past.

CCCXVII. PLEASE CLOSE THE WINDOW

Please close the window,
Also close the door.
There's a draft in here,
And it's freezing the floor.

Is it possible
It is intruding
On my Civil Rights?
Is this thing worth feuding?

Every time I try
To light a candle
The draft cones along
Like an evil vandal.

It blows out the flame
As soon as it is lit.
It is a losing war,
I am forced to admit.

I wonder, really,
If this thing is unique,
Or in a larger
Sense, would it spring a leak?

This draft thing is strange
And terribly cold.
I'm glad there's not a
Blizzard. I'm not too bold.

I can't seem to close
The door or window.
Sonder what this means.
I wonder where I'll go.

PAINTING

Look at him, looking at himself
Scared, but attempting to remain
Objective   he sits
Staring with amazement of beauty:
Innumerable tons of water
A cool lake set in tall hills,
Gentle winds brushing pictures.
He can't help but to compare,
Imagining himself one of many
A fish swims in its school,
Swimming only from bank to bank,
Always limited to lake, no stream.
Always confined to its lake-world.
"What, then, after death?"
As he observes a drying fish-carcass
Left by a sports-human
Fisherhuman of fisherhuman with hooks
Making ripples in lake-surface:
Scratches in a master painting.

GET ON YOUR SOAPBOX

Silver blade fell, slitting a cloud
Gold blade rose, slitting sea
Journey on, sweet sharp knives
Slice through undiscovered territories
Silver blade penetrating ocean and earth
Gold blade penetrating our outer space

Launch a space-craft, but stay near home
        here we expand our minds
        send mechanical voyagers

Plunger deep into our dark oceans
        Find impossible life
        pull creatures and plants home

Get on your soapbox and reach for the stars
        Sea stars and red giants
        The out-of-reach on the top shelf

How   do earth replenish itself
Does our galaxy change this way
Are   there l a w s of nature
Standard, as we know our elements
Slice, blades, slice s m oo th ly
Don't wound worlds, explore

PERFIDIOUS ALBION

Perfidious Albion drew a line across the room.
He wore suit and tie and spoke elegantly.
The room became a place of doom
To any who would not acknowledge his Presidency.
He built upon his borders with electric wire.
He guarded is side with threats of fire.
Perfidious Albion took all the credits
For prosperity, righteousness, but not the debits.
He smiles and waves and speaks of greatness,
But everything he says is bitterly tasteless.

PONDER

Silent cries for help.
Laugh when I am wrong.
Quickly grab large hand.
Take me for a ride.
Talk while music plays.
Fall (clumsily?) from
A sturdy wooden chair.
Smiles with the anger
In my heavy-brown eyes.
Stand while others sit,
Talk and ponder questions
While others draw images,
Argue loud, though
The subject is mundane.
Pout when no one is around,
And nobody has heard
The silent cries for help.

201

NATIVE INTELLIGENCE

Native intelligence relies on Common Sense,
And practiced skills handed down through generations.
Its present tense follows its past solemn tense
On this a culture finds its great foundations.

WITHOUT WARNING

The sun's rays lit the misty dawn
And drew the morning predators out.
Coyotes watch with thirst both sheep and fawn,
Attacking without warning as they scout their route.

A FRESH PAIR OF EYES

Bats in the belfry leave a stench in the room,
Guano on the rafters and the floor.
I have bigger fish to fry for whom
Jack Frost brought through the door.

RAIN ON YOUR PARADE

Right as rain and reign is right
When the sky is rainbow bright.
Take a raincheck to the bank
And they will think that it's a prank.
Fall from grace, take my advise,
You'll enter in Fool's Paradise.
Jack-of-all-trades, he clutched at straws
and got a present from Grandfather Clause.
As rare as hen's teeth,
Average Joe has a bird-brain
And way down beneath
He is sadly insane.
He's gone from rags to riches
And riches to rags.
He starves and then binges.
He sags one day and another he brags.
Drag your heels across the grass roots.
Luck of the draw stains his old boots.

Kolinahr

LIONESS

Crawl slow, Lioness.
Listen to this.
Swipe, but claws in,
Not to mark where you have been.

ISABELLE, WHEN WE WERE SIX

Isabelle said to me as we walked,
Why do you use big words?
You talk funny.

What big words? I wondered.
I inquired as to what specific vocabulary
Was for her a stumbling block.

Isabelle replied "serious."
I said that's only three syllables.
It is not any bigger than your name.

She rolled her eyes.
Or else she gazed at something in the trees
As we walked under them.

There is a plethora of life to see in the trees.
How am I to discern what words another
Knows and does not know?

I SAW HIM

I saw him in the afternoon
Upset, screaming at himself
Through his understanding father.

Black hair shone upon the air mist.
Deep soft eyes slit the sky:
Lame attraverso vino rosso sangue.
His strong body collapsed,
His questioning mind fought
For answers and life here.
Spirited hands smeared tears
From cheeks, eyes, to wind-blown hair.

I saw him in the afternoon
Upset, screaming at himself
Through his understanding father.

THE MAGICIAN STANDS

The magician stands before the audience
with a rope
an ordinary rope
nothing up the sleeves.

He ties a knot in the middle of the rope
sticks the knot in his mouth and chews,
the ends of the robe dangling
on either side of his mouth like spittle

he removes the rope from his mouth.
the knot is predictably gone. He asks,
"What is missing?"
The audience is supposed to respond,
"The knot" and obediently applaud.

They do not answer, "An automobile",
 "lavender", "my father" or "transcendence."

COLD HERE?

He looks tired, doesn't he?
Why else would his hands tremble,
                    Is it cold in here?
Fingers keep stroking back hair.
Eyebrows lean toward cheeks.
Tight pockets cling to coin-searching fingers.
The quarter falls to crash money inside machine.
Hesitation.
A nickel falls to crash money.
Wow , far-out.
Another mickle does the same.
The lever is pressed and the vegetable juice falls.
Peel off the aluminum seal.
Legs pretzel to the floor, by the wall.
Blood throbs muscles in legs.
Deep, slow, nose-breaths fill body.
Peaceful relaxation and understanding.
Occasional gulp of juice.
The humans are but echoes inside themselves.
The juice slowly disappears.

PALMS

Sun bright in palms
Back arched against green grass
Hair limp, star-like
Breezes slow, cool, brush sweat
You are young in all your
Wrinkles make a landscape
Beauty in an inner nature
You are a world your own
Modeled after a world
You must survive the fury

209

You must listen to your voice
In deep meandering canyons
You must bathe in river pools
Shower under cold falls
Swim lakes and absorb
Energy of oceans
You must run between trees
Think with life and decay
Walk smooth dry rocks, boulders of
An evaporated river, walk
Bright lit machairs, sand
Absorbing coolness of feet
You must dance in fields of
Soft grass, level land, and
Sleep there, sun in palms.

RAGING

r ^{a} gi ^{n} g ^{ri} v ^{e} r

silent

brook

PEACE AND CALM

Crying, confused, and keeping in touch
With memories and eyes that will see.
First glimpses of abstract reality:
The arrow must bend before flight.
Trying too hard to accept the posters on the wall.
Tulips begin to unfold to wind.
Cleverness spills from innocent tears.
A glass of water spills
warm sun dries.
A thorn grows from a neighbor-rose.
The thorn jabs and causes tears.
Leaves wipe tears, bandage.
Birds are pushed from nests and fly!
They fly though dreams and poetry fields.
The key has changed hands.
Longing for colors. Peace and calm are here.
By myself, alone, but not alone.
Condensation collects on the glass.
Birds hunger for food.
Humans hunger for the sea-breeze.

I STAND ALONE

I stand alone.
An endless ocean
Surrounds the peninsula
That secures me.
As I walk, slowly, cautiously,
Down the narrow land,
I am unsure,
Yet in hope for light.
The grey clouds
Are invisible
By the obscurity of night.
As I cut my foot
On a small stone
The cool wind turns cold.
It nearly freezes my warm blood,
Oozing from my foot.
The lovely stone
Is doused in sticky crimson gore.
I bleed
And yet I know that I'll heal.
But remaining there will be
A scar: a coarse reminder,
And mist on my mind.

COLLECTED

Walking back again, protecting.
Each river, flowing, is energy.
I am a composite stream,
A combination of all I've touched.
I am a cloud, collected waters.
Soar me. Watch my images.
One will see the matador,
Another will envision the breath
      of the hill.
I must re-charge of energy.

ICE-SWIRLS

Ice-swirls white and blue, melting at edges,
Branch tips, grass grows to sky.
Warm fractions molded into oneness.
Do not beat the too-incredible odds.
Search for the nourishment,
And be rewarded for troubles.
Peel off the outer shell too blinding,
Let drop the vail of modesty.

minimalism

mini
mal
ism

KARATE

                    Karate
              Life Force
          Discipline
         Exercise
     Spiritual
     Awakening
       Centering
              of one's
                    being

                    focus

                         power
                       concentrate
                        meditate
                          penetrate
                            consecrate
                          devastate
                        lung. heart.
                        soul fire
                      high peace

TEAR VISION

Symbols exchanged. Leaves of autumn
Die, crumbling. Edged grains
Cut into feet-itch, my friend, itch.
The autumn is in the other possession
      isolation
            Concentration to abstract
Avoid the inter-juxtaposition of the leaves
Fall, catching in stringed hair. Disillusion
You at to my character ... what is.
Where are my leaves? Autumn?
Winter don't disguise your ego. Edged grains
Smell of cool rain, shirt, shoes and hair
Caught hanging on my eyelids. Vision
      see the air
Don't let your mind railroad tracks fly blue-gold.
Swim in the warm mist of me. Clouds fall.
Steam rise, slow and you and I are tear.
I, too, stand amid that shore roar
        peace
     silence within thunder.

WHAT GREAT ENCHANTING SEED

What great enchanting seed has sprouted in
The harvests gained and lost, of love and time?
And what deep-rooted power grows sublime
That lures minds of great and modest myn
To dwell about its depths in mortal lust
Of understanding? Certain discipline
Invades the heart, the soul, and quiet grin
Of myn, and makes them ponder over just
And unjust laws of nature in yts prime.
There's only an unlimited distrust
In what we fail to understand. We must,
Then, reap our crop while fadeless bells still chime.
So indolent the child's mind appears,
But active it does bide amid frontiers.

WHAT HE'S DONE

We cannot blame him for what he has done.
This course of discourse was inevitable.
He's led the World to a compromise
Through something called destruction.
Too many who lived are not living.
Too many who died should live.
If I have two pair, but my friend has four
Queens, I feel he has one too-much.
We were warned, but only ignored.
Some laughed (and lied to themselves) in disbelief.
But the graves rose out from the ground,
The air breathed the hideous death,

And we cannot blame him for what he has done.
We put him in this situation ourselves (some of us).
We gave him the power he needed.
The diseased nature inside him
Supplied all the more that was needed.
Yes, He led the world to its
        destructive   climax,
But it is not fair to blame him alone for what he has done.

THE METRONOME IS

The
rigid metronome
is set to sixty-two: larghetto
His focused mind is keeping tempo
with the wind, but worlds spin 'round
their burning suns and stars move 'cross
the span and he recalls a victim of himself

218

EXPANDING

Expanding consciousness.
Elasticized concept perceptiveness.
Drag seaweed long across bridge.
Salty, green, purple-bruised weed.
Grab walls, railing, chairs.
Stare at warped paint on ceilings.
Watch the images zoom
Forward, back, within glowing
Frames, radiating, lighting
Walls arc over bent body.
Stationary flower shadows contrast light.
Green pillows, large, mother floor.
Seven trees fall from winds.
Dig up fragments from future.
Elasticized concept perceptiveness.
Connection to the universe.
Altruism through pure logic.
Expanding consciousness.

Pi

Pi
is a
great
numeral
everlasting
where Kalista may bask
but I'm a fan of primes

Epilogue

Most of these poems were inspired by events or locations in Richmond, Virginia. "Dead Steel Sheets", for example, was written while on a hike by the James River, upon finding an old rusted-out building on the banks.

This work contains various devises, including: The Fibonacci sequence, Pi, Elements from the Periodic Table, hidden phrases and Prime Numbers. They are all presented in a logical manner. I challenge you to locate these if you haven't already recognized them.

For news, book reviews and updates on my writing, please visit https://thehomesreview.blogspot.com

Poems of a Spectrum-Autist

For additional information, please visit these excellent sites.

Autism

nationalautismassociation.org

psychcentral.com/lib/adults-with-autism/

www.autism-society.org

Poetry

www.poetrysociety.org/psa

Spiritual Formation

www.spiritualityandpractice.com

www.ingramcontent.com/pod-product-compliance
Lightning Source LLC
Chambersburg PA
CBHW051720020426

42333CB00014B/1067